International Crafts and Games

By

Cynthia G. Adams

Cover and inside illustrations by

Carol Stott

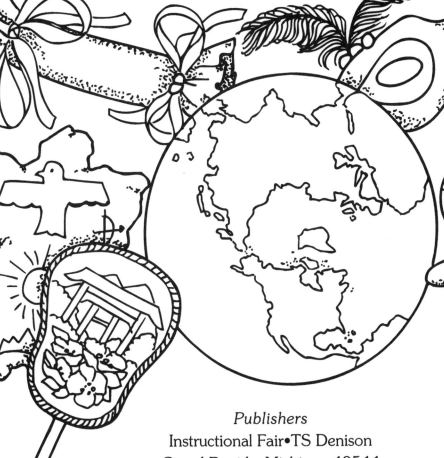

Publishers
Instructional Fair•TS Denison
Grand Rapids, Michigan 49544

Instructional Fair•TS Denison

Instructional Fair • TS Denison grants the right to the individual purchaser to reproduce patterns and student activity materials in this book for noncommercial individual or classroom use only. Reproduction for an entire school or school system is strictly prohibited. No other part of this publication may be reproduced in whole or in part. No part of this publication may be reproduced for storage in a retrieval system, or transmitted in any form or by any means, electronic, mechanical, recording, or otherwise, without the prior written permission of the publisher. For information regarding permission write to: Instructional Fair • TS Denison, P.O. Box 1650, Grand Rapids, MI 49501.

Credits

Author: Cynthia G. Adams

Cover & Inside Illustrations: Carol Stott

Project Director/Editor:
    Debra Olson Pressnall

Art Production: Darcy Bell-Myers

Typesetting: River Road Graphics

About the Author

Cynthia G. Adams, M.Ed., is a graduate of the University of Cincinnati and Xavier University in Cincinnati, Ohio. She has taught elementary music and special education in Cincinnati public schools for twenty-two years. In addition, Cynthia G. Adams has been a presenter at local thematic teaching seminars.

Standard Book Number 1-56822-526-1
International Crafts and Games
Copyright©1997 by Instructional Fair•TS Denison
2400 Turner Avenue NW
Grand Rapids, Michigan 49544

Table of Contents

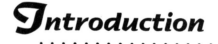

Introduction

Celebrate the rich diversity of cultures with these simple and inexpensive projects. With 100 projects from which to chose, just gather readily-available materials and follow the clear step-by-step instructions. For some crafts, you will need to make the project clay beforehand.

Project Clay
2 cups (474 mL) all-purpose flour
1 cup (237 mL) salt
½ –1 cup (118–237 mL) water
2 Tbsp. (29.6 mL) vegetable oil

Combine the ingredients in a mixing bowl and knead until smooth. Place the finished projects on waxed paper or aluminum foil (if baking them). They will air day in a few day or you may bake them at low heat.

AFRICA

Adinkra Banner

Adinkra is a method of stamping fabric with symbolic religious and cultural motifs. It has been a tradition of the Ashanti tribe in Ghana since the 19th century.

Materials Needed

- ❏ Styrofoam blocks of various sizes to make stamps
- ❏ pencil
- ❏ craft stick
- ❏ plastic knife or tools for cutting
- ❏ acrylic paint (black, red, green, yellow)
- ❏ paintbrushes or brayer
- ❏ Plexiglass
- ❏ white cotton sheet
- ❏ lightweight dowel (18" or 457 mm in length)
- ❏ cord or yarn

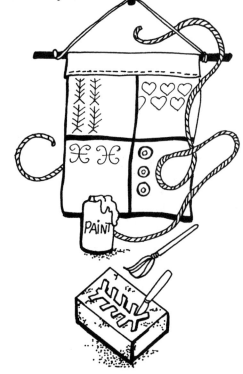

Directions

1. Cut a 15" x 20" (381 x 508 mm) rectangle from the white cotton sheet. Be sure one short edge of the rectangle includes part of the hem of the sheet (or sew the edge to make a flap). Keep this edge intact to hold the dowel stick.

2. Use the tools to cut symbols in the foam blocks. Make several designs if you wish. (See diagrams.)

3. Brush paint lightly onto stamps or apply paint with a brayer. (To use the brayer, squirt a small amount of paint on the Plexiglass and roll the brayer through the paint. Then roll the brayer across the stamp.) Use different colors for each stamp.

4. Press the painted stamp on the cloth. Allow the paint to dry.

5. Hang the banner by inserting the dowel stick in the hem of the sheet. Tie the cord or yarn to the dowel for hanging the banner.

Note: Prints may also be made on paper.

 royalty

 independence

 hope

 strength

 patience and endurance

 praise

 security and safety in home

 good luck

Akua-Ba Doll

These dolls are tucked in the waistbands of Ashanti women. They believe the dolls will cause their unborn children to be beautiful and perfectly formed. Young girls who hope to have children in the future also carry the Akua-Ba dolls.

Materials Needed

- ❏ project clay (recipe p. 4)
- ❏ patterns on page 8
- ❏ heavy cardboard
- ❏ yarn or string
- ❏ scissors
- ❏ pencil
- ❏ small tube macaroni and/or beads
- ❏ needle and thread

Directions

1. Enlarge the head pattern 130%.
2. Tape the head pattern onto the doll's body. Cut the doll from heavy cardboard.
3. Using the pattern, form a doll from the clay.
4. Mark the face with a pencil. If you wish, make holes in the ears to hold earrings. Allow the clay to air dry or bake it at 350° until browned (about 15 minutes).
5. When the doll feels cool, make earrings by stringing small beads with the needle and thread and then attach them at the ears.
6. Make two necklaces from beads, macaroni and yarn or string. Tie them at the doll's neck and waist.

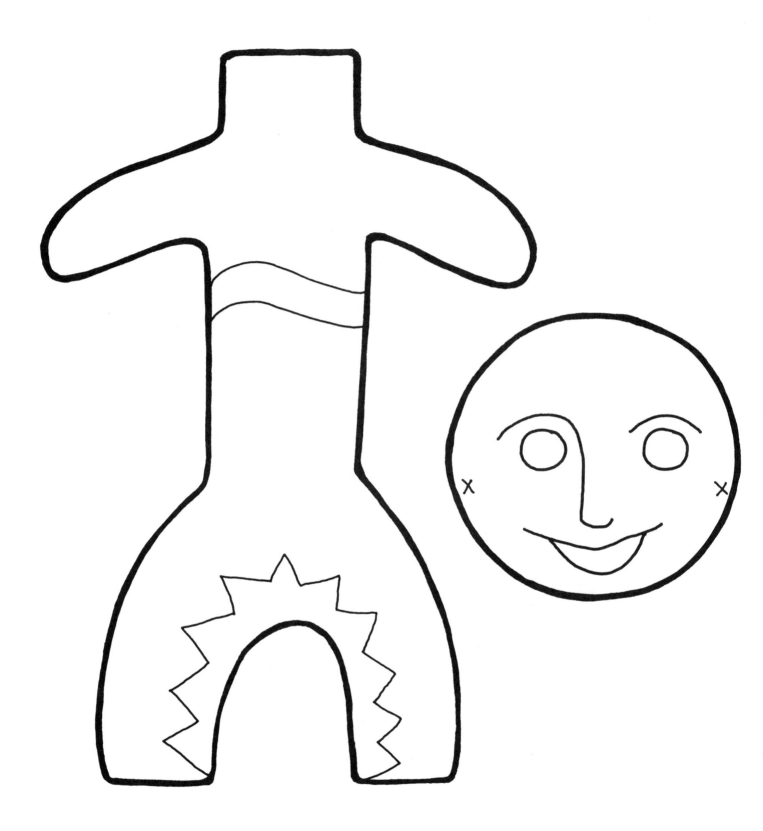

Crocodile

The people of Baule believe a legend that says crocodiles lined up side by side so that their people could cross a river to safety from the warring Ashanti. The crocodile with a fish in its mouth is a sacred symbol to them.

Materials Needed

- ☐ butcher (brown) paper
- ☐ orange construction paper
- ☐ newspaper
- ☐ markers
- ☐ pencil
- ☐ glue
- ☐ scissors
- ☐ stapler

Directions

1. Draw a large crocodile on the butcher paper. Cut two of the same shape.
2. Decorate each side with markers.
3. Staple the crocodiles together around the edges leaving an opening at the top.
4. Tear the newspaper into small pieces and crumple it into balls. Stuff the newspaper into the crocodile and staple the top opening closed.
5. Design a fish from the orange construction paper and decorate it with markers.
6. Glue the fish to the crocodile's mouth.

Dashiki

Men of West Africa wear these simple, brightly colored, traditional shirts. In some cities, a sidewalk tailor will make a dashiki while you wait.

Materials Needed

- ☐ fabric, about 36" x 48" (91 x 122 cm) in size
- ☐ scissors
- ☐ needle
- ☐ thread
- ☐ ruler or measuring tape

Directions

Note: You may wish to tie-dye the fabric before-hand.

1. Fold the fabric in half (horizontally) and then in half again (vertically).

2. Cut a circular opening about 4" (102 mm) down for the neckline.

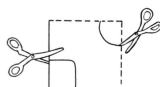

3. Cut along the sides and shape the sleeves as shown.

4. Open the fabric and stitch the sides shut, leaving the armhole open.

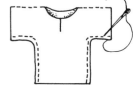

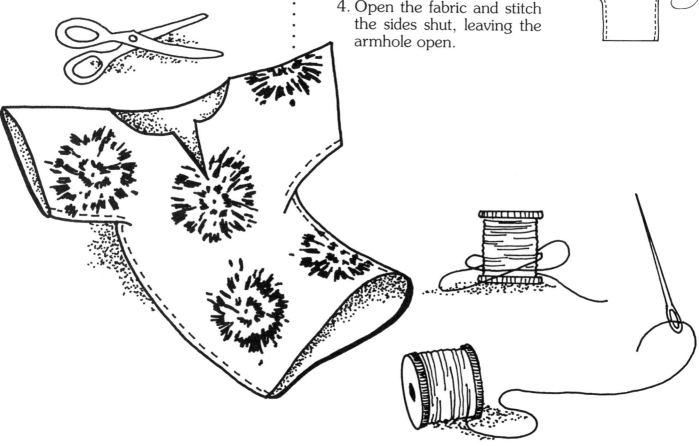

Double Drum

Skillful drummers can produce many interesting sounds from these double-headed drums. They may be made of wood, clay, bone, or metal. Drumheads are usually animal skins.

Materials Needed

- ☐ two clay flower pots (5"–6" or 127–152 cm in diameter)
- ☐ glue
- ☐ masking tape
- ☐ bongo drumheads (from a music store)
- ☐ scissors
- ☐ strong cord
- ☐ hole punch
- ☐ basin of water
- ☐ newspaper
- ☐ brown paint
- ☐ flour and water mixture (one part flour, two parts water)
- ☐ wooden or plastic bead and stick for drumstick

Directions

1. Glue the flower pot bottoms together.
2. Tear the newspaper into thin strips and soak them in the flour and water mixture.
3. Shape a layer of newspaper strips around the pots.
4. Allow the paper to dry thoroughly.
5. Paint the papier mâché light brown.
6. Soak the drumheads in water until they are pliable.
7. Drain the excess water and shape the drumhead around the top pot.
8. Measure and cut a circle from the drumhead about 2" (51 mm) wider in diameter than the top of the pot.
9. Punch holes in the circumference of the drumhead and lay it aside.
10. Repeat the previous steps to prepare the other drumhead.
11. Cover both ends of the flower pots with the drumheads. Lace the circles together (see diagram), tightening as you pull on the laces.
12. Make a drumstick with a wooden or plastic bead on the end of a stick. *Note:* For a softer sound, wrap your stick with yarn.

Folding Fan

African fans are made of many different materials—bark, leather, and wood. They are decorated with leather lacing, embroidery, and beads. Large ceremonial fans keep kings cool when they hold court and receive their subjects.

Materials Needed

- ☐ white paper, 6" x 72" (15 x 183 cm) in size
- ☐ markers
- ☐ two lightweight wooden rulers or paint stirring sticks
- ☐ glue
- ☐ stapler
- ☐ masking tape
- ☐ 12" (305 mm) length of ribbon or yarn
- ☐ pictures of traditional fans

Directions

1. Decorate the paper with markers. Use earth colors for the decoration. *Note:* Keep in mind how the folds will affect the drawing.
2. Fold the length of paper in 2" (51 mm) wide accordion folds.
3. Hold the folds closed and staple three times across the top of the fan very near the edge.
4. Cover the staples with masking tape.
5. Glue the ribbon near the bottom on one side of the folded fan.
6. Glue one ruler on each side of the accordion folds.
7. Tie the fan open with the ribbon.

Friction Drum

Friction drums may be made from any container that can be tightly covered. The tops are pierced and a stick is inserted through the center. Sounds vibrate from the drum when the stick is rubbed around or up and down.

Materials Needed

- ❏ oatmeal box with a lid
- ❏ dowel stick (½" or 13 mm in width and about 6" or 152 mm taller than the box)
- ❏ construction paper
- ❏ tempera paint
- ❏ glue (optional)
- ❏ scissors
- ❏ pictures of friction drums
- ❏ masking tape

Directions

1. Decorate the body of the drum as you wish with construction paper or paints.
2. Make a small hole in the lid. Tape the lid securely to the box.
3. Insert the dowel stick.

Galimoto

Galimoto is the name given a push toy made by the children of Malawi. The children shape all kinds of found objects into cars, trucks, bicycles, trains, or helicopters.

Materials Needed

- ☐ chenille stems or wire
- ☐ cardboard
- ☐ scissors
- ☐ string or yarn
- ☐ long straight stick
- ☐ pictures of vehicles

Directions

1. Provide pictures of a variety of vehicles. Point out the shapes that are predominate in each one.
2. Encourage the students to use the supplies to create some type of galimoto.

Note: The stick will become the handle for the finished push toy.

Hammered Metal Picture

Nigerian craftsmen hammer pictures onto sheets of lightweight metal.
They also design jewelry and sculptures from metals.

Materials Needed

- ❏ roll of aluminium flashing (available at a building supply store)
- ❏ tin snips
- ❏ masking tape
- ❏ patterns on pages 16 and 17
- ❏ hammer, screwdriver, dull nail(s)
- ❏ cardboard
- ❏ X-acto knife

Directions

1. Cut the tin sheet to a desired size and cover the edges with masking tape.
2. Choose one of the animals for your design and draw it on the tin. Use the tools to gently hammer along the shape. **Do not** break through the tin. Gently tap a nail to make each eye. Use the screwdriver to make the outline of the animal and additional lines for details on the body.
3. When the lines of the picture are finished, carefully hammer out the entire background.
4. Cut a cardboard frame at least 3" (76 mm) larger than your picture. Ask an adult to cut slits in the corners as shown.
5. Remove the tape from the edges of the tin sheet.
6. Frame and hang your picture.

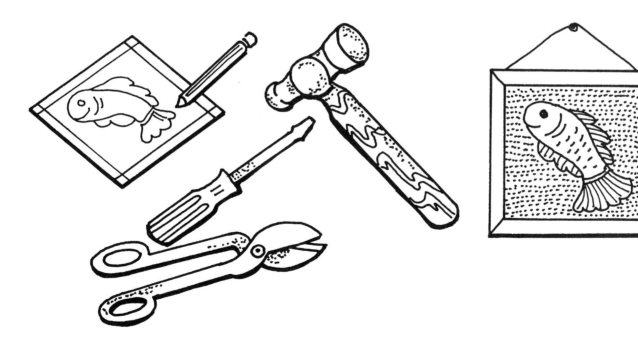

Harvest Doll

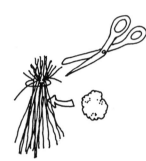

These figures, made in different ways all over the world, are believed to hold the spirits living in plants. They are made from the last wheat or bundle of grass and kept through the winter until the next planting season. In some cultures, the doll is planted with the next crop.

Materials Needed

- ☐ bundle of grasses (wheat or straw)
- ☐ wire or string
- ☐ cotton balls
- ☐ scissors

Directions

1. Wire the bundle tightly at the top.
2. Trim the grasses neatly, just above the wire.
3. Insert some cotton and tie or wire at the neck.
4. Insert some short grasses under the chin and tie off. These will become the arms.
5. Separate the remaining length into two bunches and tie them to make the legs or allow the remaining length to hang like a skirt.

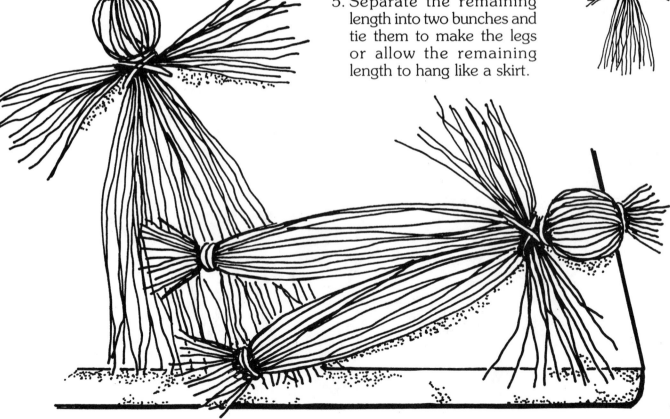

Mancala

This board game is played all over Africa (also in parts of the West Indies, in Guyana and Sri Lanka). The rules differ somewhat in different sections of the continent. It is called Oware in the west and Ohoro in the south. Sometimes people simply make twelve holes in the sand and play wherever they are.

Materials Needed

- ☐ cardboard egg carton
- ☐ two small Styrofoam cups
- ☐ scissors
- ☐ tempera paints
- ☐ varnish (optional)
- ☐ masking tape
- ☐ 48 dried beans

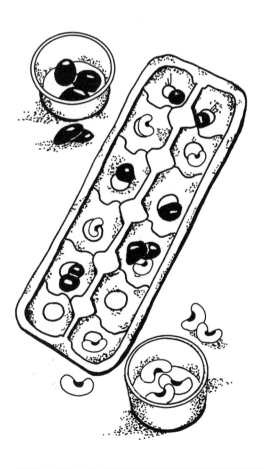

Directions

1. Cut off the lid of the carton.
2. Glue the base inside the lid.
3. Trim the cups to 2" (51 mm) in height.
4. Paint all of the board pieces beige with green, black, and red designs.

Optional: Varnish the game board.

How to Play (A Simplified Version)

1. Player A will use the right side of the board; Player B will play the left. Each player will have a cup (bank) to hold the captured beans.
2. Start by placing four beans in each hole on the game board.
3. To begin the game, Player A will take four beans from any hole on the right side and place one bean in each of the next four holes, moving counterclockwise around the board. When the last bean is put into a hole, all five of those beans are picked up and placed in Player A's bank.
4. Play continues until the last bean falls into an **empty** hole.
5. At that point, Player B begins by taking four beans from a space on the left side of the board. Play proceeds as above.
6. The game continues until all of the beans have been collected.
7. The player with the most beans is the winner.

Nine Men's Morris

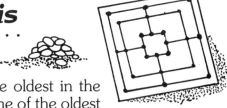

This ancient board game for two players is one of the oldest in the world. Found *everywhere from Sri Lanka to Norway*, one of the oldest boards is from an Egyptian temple built in 1,400 B.C.

Materials Needed

☐ pattern on page 21
☐ markers or crayons
☐ scissors
☐ tagboard
☐ glue
☐ two sets of nine game pieces

Directions

1. Photocopy the game board on page 21 and decorate it with markers.
2. Glue the game board to tagboard.

How to Play

1. Select game pieces for two players.
2. To begin play, each player takes a turn placing one marker on the game board.
3. The object is to set three markers in a row to form a *mill*.
4. When a player completes a mill that player may remove one of the other player's markers from the board. *Remember:* Markers in a mill are safe and cannot be removed.
5. When all of the markers are placed on the board, the players take turns moving one marker one point in any direction trying to form mills. *Remember:* Whenever a mill is made, remove one the opponent's markers from the board.
6. The game is over when one player has only two remaining pieces on the board.

Sacred Cat

The ancient Egyptians kept cats as pets as early as 2100 B.C. By 450 B.C. cats had become a protected, sacred animal. For religious reasons, ancient Egyptians had cats mummified and entombed in a special cemetery.

Materials Needed

- ☐ paper towel tube
- ☐ scissors
- ☐ project clay (p. 4)
- ☐ tempera paint or markers
- ☐ cloth (torn in strips)
- ☐ glue or wallpaper paste
- ☐ paintbrush

Directions

1. Form a cat head from the project clay.
2. Hollow out the center as much as possible and set the head aside to dry.
3. Cut 2" (51 mm) slits around one end of the tube.
4. Squeeze the slit end together and force it into the cat's head.
5. Coat the "neck" area with additional clay. Allow the clay to dry.
6. Paint the cat's head and neck. Add the facial features.
7. Wrap the tube with cloth strips that are coated with thinned glue or wallpaper paste.
8. Allow the model to dry.

Serpent Game

Early Egyptians played many games using dice and marbles. The original serpent games were sculptured from alabaster.

Materials Needed

- ☐ cardboard circle
  (8" or 203 mm in diameter)
- ☐ game board pattern on page 25
- ☐ small Styrofoam cup
- ☐ glue
- ☐ crayons
- ☐ die and coins or beans

Directions

1. Photocopy the game board pattern.
2. Color the boxes marked with an "X" turquoise blue.
3. Decorate the serpent's head and tail.
4. Cut out the game board and glue it to the cardboard circle.
5. Glue the Styrofoam cup to the bottom as shown.

How to Play

1. Each player selects a game piece.
2. To begin play, the first player throws the die and moves the game piece the correct number of spaces, beginning after the serpent's tail. Then the other player takes a turn.
3. Play continues as the players take turns moving the game pieces.
4. If a game piece lands in a box where there is another marker, the player must move the game piece **back** seven spaces.
5. If the game piece lands in a colored box, the player moves the game piece ahead to the next colored box.
6. The game ends when a player rolls the exact number of spaces to move inside the serpent's head. If a number higher than the distance to the head is rolled, the player must move the game piece back that number of boxes.

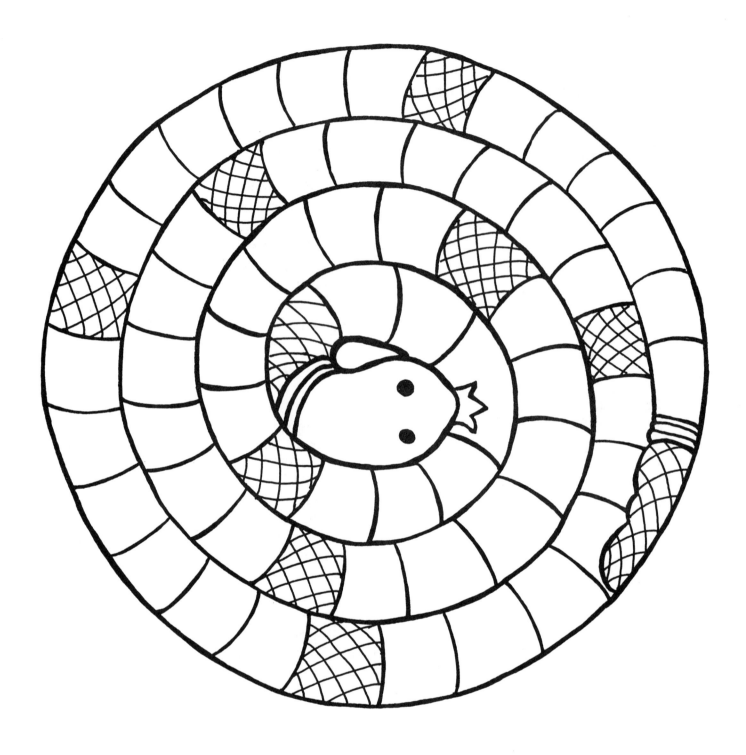

Shield

African shields come in a variety of sizes and shapes. They are made from animal skins stretched on a frame. Some very small shields are used symbolically in dance rituals.

Materials Needed

- ☐ large plastic lid or cardboard circle
- ☐ sharp scissors
- ☐ construction paper scraps
- ☐ glue
- ☐ heavy string
- ☐ pictures of African shields

Directions

1. Decorate the front of the lid with colorful paper designs. Refer to reference material for ideas.

2. Use the scissors to make two holes at the top and bottom of the lid.

3. Thread the string through the holes, cross the ends, and tie them securely in the back to make a handle.

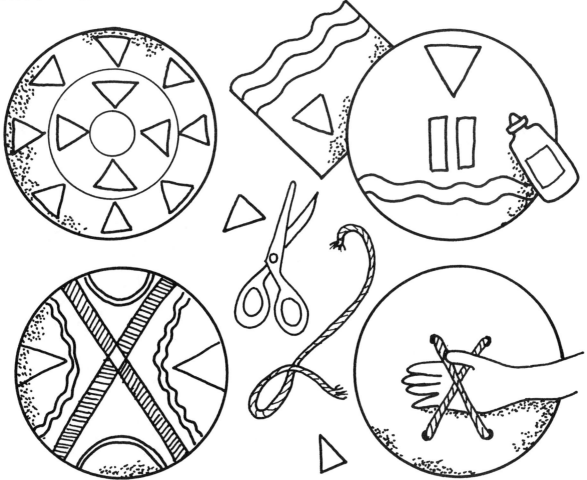

Sistrum

The sistrum, a U-shaped rattle, was an important instrument in ancient Egypt. It was played by the priests and priestesses during worship ceremonies. When it was shaken, the metal disks produced a pleasant jingling sound.

Materials Needed

- ❑ coat hanger
- ❑ wire cutter
- ❑ pliers
- ❑ picture wire
- ❑ 20 or more metal washers
- ❑ duct tape

Directions

1. Cut a length of coat hanger wire and bend it into a U-shape. Use the pliers to twist about 4" (102 mm) together for a handle.

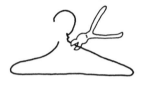

2. Wrap several layers of duct tape around the handle.

3. Attach three or four lengths of picture wire around the coat hanger frame (in figure eights).

4. Thread the washers onto each wire.

5. Twist the ends of the wire together tightly.

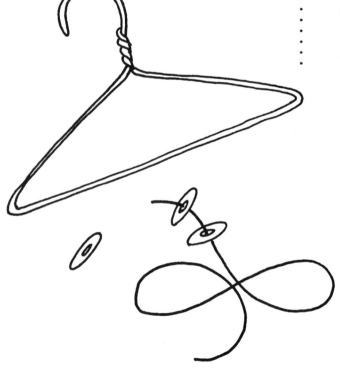

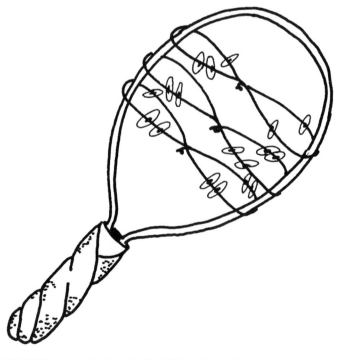

Sotho Beaded Doll

When a Sotho woman marries, she carries a magic doll. The name she gives this doll is also the name she will give her first child. The doll is cone shaped and has no arms or legs.

Materials Needed

- ❏ white tagboard
  (12" x 18" or 305 x 457 mm)
- ❏ markers
- ❏ stapler
- ❏ scissors
- ❏ white glue
- ❏ small plastic beads and sequins

Directions

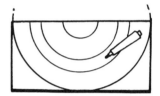

1. Cut the tagboard into a half circle.
2. Color rows of beads along the curved edge of the half circle. Continue the rows to cover about two thirds of the shape.
3. Draw a face and hair in the center of the remaining space.
4. Form the tagboard into a cone and staple shut.
5. Glue beads and sequins randomly in the beaded section of the doll.

Tie-Dye Fabric

The tie-dye method has been practiced around the world for hundreds of years. The people of the Baule and Yoruba tribes use this method to create interesting patterns on cloth.

Materials Needed

- ☐ 10" (254 mm) square of white cotton cloth
- ☐ various natural objects (rocks, sticks, etc.)
- ☐ package string
- ☐ indigo (dark blue) fabric dye
- ☐ large basin
- ☐ rags
- ☐ iron
- ☐ rubber gloves

Directions

1. Fold and wrap the fabric around natural items as you wish.
2. Wrap some string around each one and fasten with knots. *Note:* The cloth will resist the dye under the string.
3. Prepare the dye according to directions on the package.
4. Dip sections of your fabric into the dye. Blot excess dye on the rags.
5. Allow the fabric to dry.
6. Cut off the string and then iron your cloth flat.
7. If possible, experiment with several designs.

Tribal Beads

Beads may be worn as jewelry, or used for prayers and trading. They are made of materials like clay, glass, bone, and precious metals.

Materials Needed

- ☐ natural sand
- ☐ white glue
- ☐ plastic spoon and bowl
- ☐ knitting needle
- ☐ plastic tray
- ☐ tempera paint
- ☐ materials for decoration (seeds, glitter)
- ☐ string or yarn
- ☐ pictures of traditional beads

Directions

1. Mix the sand and glue to make a stiff dough.
2. Pinch off enough dough to roll into a bead. (If the dough is too soft, add more sand and mix again.) Try making oval-shaped and flat, round beads.
3. Poke a hole in each bead with the knitting needle.
4. Arrange beads on the tray and allow them to dry overnight.
5. Paint the beads if you wish. Decorate some beads with glitter or glue on small seeds. If interested, refer to reference materials to view how African beaded jewelry looks.
6. Thread the beads onto the string and tie a knot. *Note:* Try making patterns combining washers, macaroni, and beads.

Warrior Mask

Some large masks actually were worn above the head with the body completely covered by grasses or cloth. Some of the most sacred masks were about 4" (102 mm) high, worn by young men after being initiated into manhood.

Materials Needed

- [ ] large cardboard box
- [ ] X-acto knife (or sharp scissors)
- [ ] glue
- [ ] paint or markers
- [ ] beads
- [ ] yarn or long grasses
- [ ] elastic
- [ ] reference books on masks

Directions

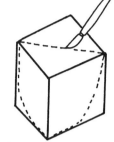

1. Cut the corner from a cardboard box as shown. Make sure that it is big enough to fit over your face.
2. Cut two holes for the eyes.
3. Draw (or paint) the remaining features.
4. Glue on beads as teeth and decorations at the hairline.
5. If you wish, make holes and string beads as earrings.
6. Add yarn or grasses for hair.
7. Make two small holes in the sides and attach the elastic.

Optional: Encourage the children to research traditional masks. Note the colors and markings that are used to decorate them.

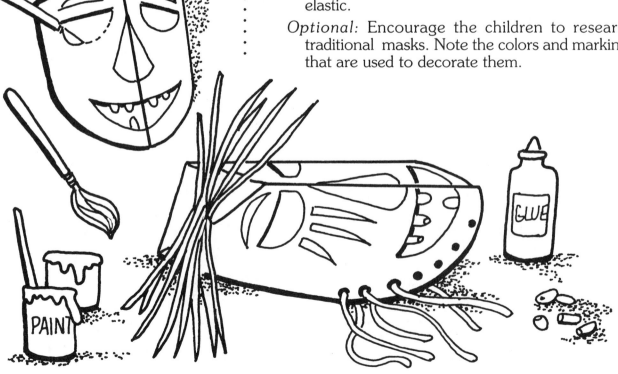

Woven Blanket

Throughout the countries south of the Sahara Desert, you will find weavers working with yarn to create belts and blankets. In Cameroon, weavings with colorful stripes that run the length of the weave can be seen.

Materials Needed

- ☐ clean Styrofoam tray
- ☐ scissors
- ☐ blue and white yarn
- ☐ hair pin
- ☐ masking tape

Directions

1. Cut notches about 1/2" (13 mm) apart across the top and bottom of the tray.

2. Cut one notch in the middle of each side to anchor the yarn at the start and finish of the project.

3. Cut pieces of blue and white yarn the same length and the board and connect them to make one length. Insert the end of yarn in the right side notch and lace it up and down through all the top and bottom notches. (This becomes the warp threads of your weaving project.) Anchor the end of the yarn in the left side notch and cut.

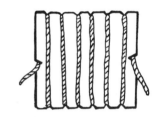

4. Cut another length of white yarn. Tie it securely to the hair pin and tape the yarn in place.

5. Weave it over and under across the warp threads. Push each row down tightly, turning the loom (or changing hands) to reverse the direction of weaving.

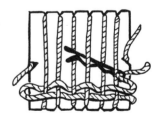

6. Continue until the weaving is complete, attaching additional yarn with a knot when needed.

7. When the weaving is finished, turn the loom over and cut through the center of the back yarn.

8. Knot the end fringe. (See diagram.)

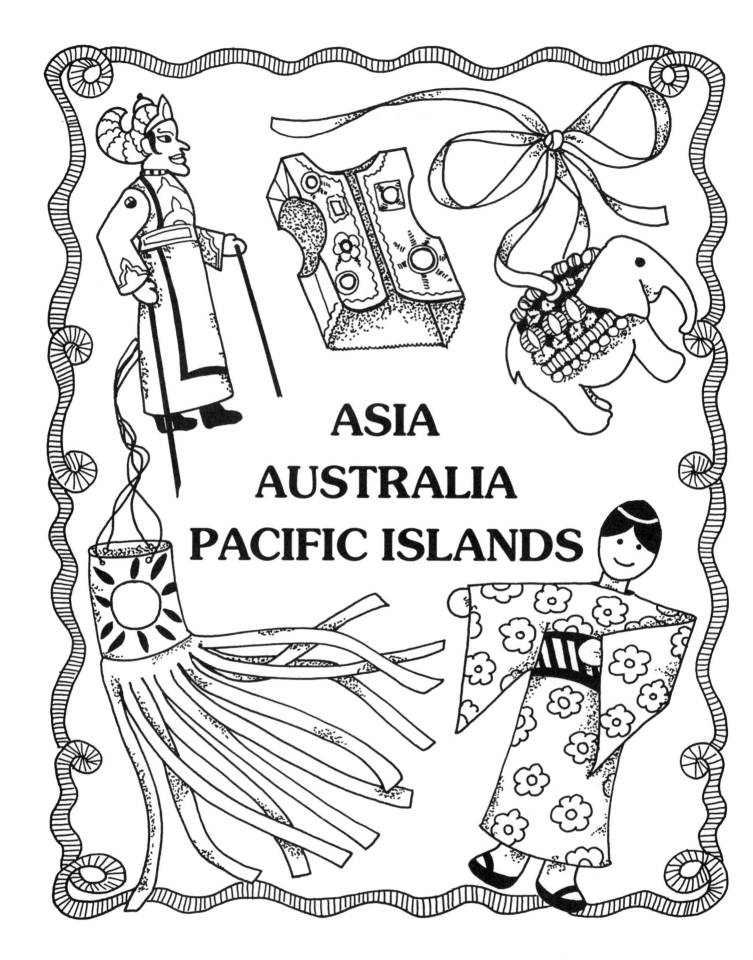

ASIA
AUSTRALIA
PACIFIC ISLANDS

Aboriginal Painting

The traditional art of Australia's Aborigines was painted on tree bark or carved in stone. It usually showed detailed designs of people and animals, representing the Aborigines' interest in nature.

Materials Needed

- ☐ large paper grocery bag (brown)
- ☐ heavy black marker
- ☐ pencil
- ☐ brown, black, and white tempera paint
- ☐ three paintbrushes
- ☐ three paint dishes
- ☐ old combs (two or three different sizes of teeth)
- ☐ newspaper
- ☐ reference books on Aboriginal paintings

Directions

1. Cover the work surface with newspaper.
2. Tear an irregular shape from the brown paper.
3. Plan a design that covers the entire paper, leaving some large open spaces to be painted. Make the drawing in pencil.
4. Mix at least three shades of brown and/or black.
5. Carefully paint within the pencil lines, one section at a time. Run a comb through the wet paint to make a striped pattern. Allow each section to dry before painting the next one. Try to play your use of paint so that the colors are different in adjacent sections.
6. When the painting is dry, trace over the pencil lines with the black marker.

Chop

Many times a person will use a personal seal, called a chop, in place of writing his/her name. The chop is inked and stamped on documents requiring a signature.

Materials Needed

- ☐ small block of wood (about 1½" or 38 mm square)
- ☐ heavy rubber bands
- ☐ pencil
- ☐ white glue
- ☐ scissors
- ☐ inked stamp pad or thinned tempera paint in a flat dish

Directions

1. Plan a design that can be made from strips of rubber bands.
2. Draw it on the wood block.
3. Cut and glue the rubber bands in place. Allow the glue to dry.
4. Press the stamp onto an ink pad and then leave your "mark" on personal items.

Daruma

These dolls come in many styles, but all are short, fat, and have no arms or legs. Legend says that Dharma, the founder of Zen Buddhism, spent nine years in meditation during which time he lost the use of his arms and legs. At the beginning of a project or when a wish is made, one eye is painted on the doll. When the project is complete or the wish comes true the second eye is added.

Materials Needed

- ☐ clean, plastic jar with lid
- ☐ acrylic paint
- ☐ paintbrush
- ☐ colored construction paper or fabric scraps

Directions

1. Put a sheet of crumpled construction paper (or the fabric) inside the jar.
2. Screw on the lid. The lid is the base of your doll.
3. Paint hair and a face (with **one** eye) on the front of your doll. Add the second eye when your wish comes true!

PAINT

Diwali Festival Lamp

Diwali, the festival of lights, is a time of joy and happiness in India. Depending on the Hindu calendar, the festival is held in October or November. Small earthenware bowls are filled with oil and wicks. These *dipa* lights are lit in front of a home altar. Many lamps are placed on the edges of the roofs of buildings at dusk.

Materials Needed

- ❐ small, clean, flat can (tuna fish or sardines)
- ❐ project clay (p. 4)
- ❐ glue
- ❐ small candle or votive
- ❐ plastic knife and other clay tools (for making designs)
- ❐ gold spray enamel

Directions

1. Flatten the clay and mold it evenly around the can.
2. Smooth the clay and use modeling tools to decorate it.
3. Make a candle holder from a band of clay. Allow it to dry.
4. Glue the candle holder on the inside of the bottom of the can as shown.
5. Spray the entire lamp with gold paint. Insert a candle.

Caution: Remind students to have an adult light the candle at home.

Dragon Boat

The Chinese Dragon Boat Festival features races between brightly colored boats decorated with dragon's heads and tails. The festival is based on the story of Qu Yuan, a poet who drowns himself to protest an unfair ruler. The villagers raced their boats across the river to save Qu Yuan, but they were too late.

Materials Needed

- ☐ 6" (152 mm) square of green construction paper
- ☐ scissors
- ☐ patterns on page 38
- ☐ glue or transparent tape
- ☐ construction paper scraps
- ☐ markers or crayons

Directions

1. Fold the boat (see diagram) from the green construction paper. Glue or tape the ends together.

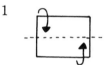
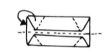

2. Color the dragon's head and tail.
3. Cut them out, and glue the two head pieces and the two tail pieces back to back.
4. Finish the boat, by gluing the head and tail to it.
5. Decorate the boat (body) with colored paper scraps.

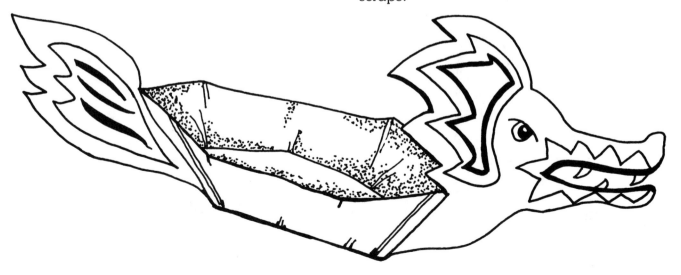

Dreidel

The dreidel became a popular Hanukkah game among Jewish children during the Middle Ages. The Hebrew letters on the dreidel stand for "a great miracle happened there (nes gadol hayah sham)." The four-sided top is usually made of wood, but elaborate ones may be made of silver or ivory.

Materials Needed

- ❑ cardboard egg carton
- ❑ markers
- ❑ scissors
- ❑ 4" (102 mm) dowel
- ❑ white glue
- ❑ pencil sharpener

 nun

 gimel

he

 shin

Directions

1. Cut out one section of the egg carton.
2. Use a black marker to write one of the Hebrew letters on each side of the dreidel (see diagram).
3. Sharpen a point on the dowel with a pencil sharpener.
4. Poke the dowel through a small hole in the bottom of the egg carton.
5. Apply glue around the dowel to hold the egg carton in place.

How to Play

The Hebrew letters stand for the English words, "nothing," "get," "half," and "share." Each player begins with a pile of nuts or small candies and contributes an agreed upon amount to the kitty. Players spin the dreidel in turn and play according to whatever letter is on the top when the dreidel falls.

- •*Shin*—nothing happens (it is a passed turn);
- •*Gimel*—the player gets all of the kitty and everyone must contribute more;
- •*He*—the player gets half of the kitty; and
- •*Shin*—the player forfeits an agreed amount to the kitty.

The game is over when all players have had enough. The winner is the player who wins the most.

Elephant Pendant

The Kashmir region of India is known for its precious stones and beautiful jewelry.

Materials Needed

- ❐ large silver sequins
- ❐ small white and blue beads
- ❐ project clay (p. 4)
- ❐ knitting needle
- ❐ silver paint
- ❐ black ribbon (¼" or 6 mm in width) or gold gift wrap cord
- ❐ glue

Directions

1. Form the clay into an elephant shape about ½" (13 mm) thick. You may use the pattern below as a guide.

2. Use a knitting needle to make a small hole in the top of the elephant's back.

3. Press the sequins and beads into the elephant's back to make a blanket. Allow the clay to dry completely. Glue the sequins and beads if needed.

4. Paint the pendant, being careful not to get any paint on the beads. String the pendant onto the ribbon to wear.

Rigid Fan

Folding and rigid fans are important to Japanese culture. Ancient Japanese used them in religious ceremonies. Warriors, rulers, and actors also use fans. They are often given as gifts.

Materials Needed

- ☐ pattern on page 42
- ☐ glue
- ☐ lightweight tagboard
- ☐ markers
- ☐ optional: feathers, glitter, sequins
- ☐ a lightweight wooden ruler or paint stirring stick
- ☐ masking tape

Directions

1. Potocopy the pattern. Color and cut out the fan.
2. Glue the fan to tagboard for stability. Cut around the shape. *Optional:* Decorate the fan with glitter, feathers, and/or sequins.
3. Glue the ruler (handle) in place about halfway up the back of the fan.
4. Wrap the handle with masking tape.

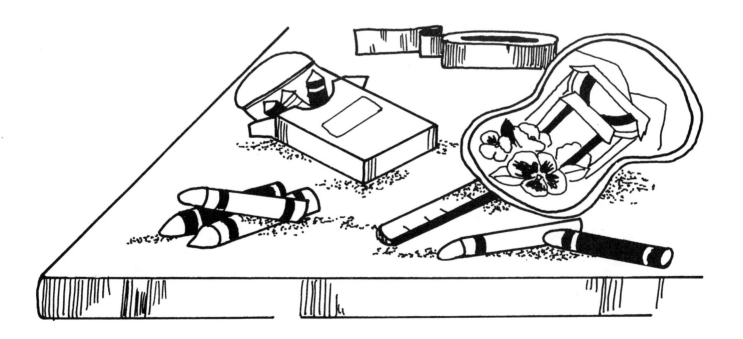

Flying Fish Kite

On May 5 (Children's Day) in Japan, a carp kite is flown for each child in the family. The carp symbolizes strength and courage and success in life.

Materials Needed

- ❏ two sheets of white construction paper (12" x 18" or 305 x 457 mm)
- ❏ markers or crayons
- ❏ chenille stem or wire, 12" (305 mm) in length
- ❏ masking tape
- ❏ white glue
- ❏ 36" (91 cm) of string, cut into thirds
- ❏ a broomstick or yardstick

Directions

1. Cut two identical long, thin fish shapes from the papers.
2. Decorate them with the markers.
3. Glue the two fish together along the top edge.
4. Fold about 1" (25 mm) of paper at the mouth into the fish.
5. Insert the chenille inside the fold. Glue or tape it firmly in place, leaving an end of the wire hanging out each side. (This wire will form the round mouth).
6. Fold the wire and glue the bottom edge of the fish closed, leaving the tail open.
7. Allow the glue to dry.
8. Twist the wire ends together and form the mouth into a circle.
9. Attach the strings at the mouth and tie them to the broomstick.

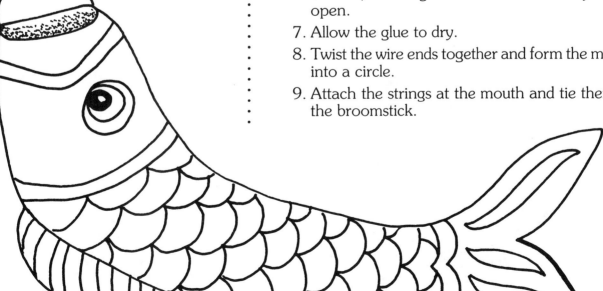

Israel

Grogger

The Purim celebration honors Esther, who long ago spoke to the king, Mordecai, and saved the Jews from being killed by a wicked man named Haman. On the eve of Purim as the Book of Esther is read in the synagogues, children rattle their noisemakers at every mention of Haman's name.

Materials Needed

- ☐ sturdy cardboard food package, about 5" x 7" x 1 1/4" (127 x 178 x 32 mm) in size
- ☐ heavy tagboard scrap
- ☐ sharp scissors
- ☐ unsharpened pencil
- ☐ hole punch
- ☐ masking tape
- ☐ colored paper
- ☐ markers
- ☐ glue
- ☐ disposable foil baking pan
- ☐ stapler

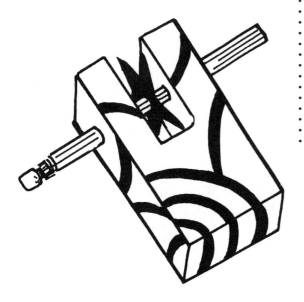

Directions

1. Remove **only** the top from the box, leaving all the flaps in place.
2. Cut 1" (25 mm) square sections from the bottom and sides of the box. (This will help amplify the sound).
3. Trace the pattern for the wheel on tagboard and cut it out. Punch a hole in the center.
4. Measure in about an inch (25 mm) from one of the top corners of the box. (Be sure the distance will make it possible for the wheel to touch the flaps).
5. Punch a hole in the top and bottom of the box.
6. Cut a 1" x 2" (25 x 51 mm) piece from the disposable foil baking pan.
7. Fold the foil over the box flap that will contact the wheel. Trim excess if needed.
8. Staple the foil over the flap.
9. Cover the box with colored paper and decorate it with markers.
10. Insert the pencil through the top hole, the center of the wheel and finally the bottom hole.
11. Tape the wheel firmly to the pencil. Twirl the pencil "handle" and listen!

Hand of Fatima

People in the Middle East believe that they will be protected from harm by wearing this good luck charm. Fatima was the daughter of the prophet Muhammed. In Iran, the Moslems call the charm the Hand of Fatima.

Materials Needed

☐ chenille stem
☐ 36" (914 mm) of narrow ribbon or yarn

Directions

1. Bend the pipe cleaner into an abstract shape of a tiny hand.
2. Divide the ribbon in half and tie the center securely to the hand. Tie the loose ends in a knot and wear your good luck charm around your neck.

Japanese Lantern

The Lantern Festival is celebrated throughout Japan. Many styles of giant lanterns illuminate the streets.

Materials Needed

- ❒ 9" x 12" (229 x 305 mm) red construction paper
- ❒ 9" x 12" (229 x 305 mm) white construction paper
- ❒ glue
- ❒ stapler
- ❒ sharp scissors
- ❒ pencil
- ❒ red or white crepe paper
- ❒ four 18" (457 mm) lengths of string
- ❒ hole punch

Directions

1. Draw some Japanese designs (characters or rising sun) on one of the papers.
2. Cut out the designs, keeping the paper intact.

3. Glue the contrasting paper behind the paper with the cutout designs. Allow to dry.
4. Roll the papers into a cylinder. Glue and staple to hold securely.
5. Cut a piece of crepe paper long enough to go around the lantern. Fringe the crepe paper within 1" (25 mm) of one end.
6. Glue the crepe paper in place around the bottom of the lantern.
7. Punch four holes in the top and hang from strings.

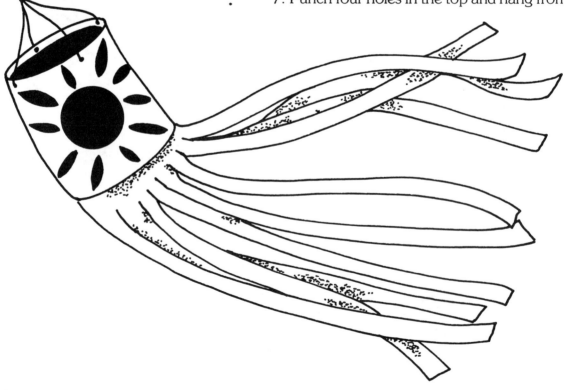

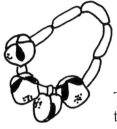

Jingles

Traditional Indian dancers call attention to their movements with these tiny bells called jingles. They are worn at the neck, ankles, and wrists.

Materials Needed

- ❐ several jingle bells (variety of small sizes)
- ❐ beads or shaped pasta
- ❐ elastic, ½" (13 mm) in width
- ❐ scissors

Directions

1. Cut the elastic long enough to fit your ankles or wrists.
2. Thread on bells, beads, or pasta and tie a knot.
3. Put them on and listen to yourself jingle!

Kai-awase

This game was originally made from the two parts of bivalve shells. The halves of each shell were split apart and put with others on a table. The object was to match the two halves again. They are beautifully painted with scenes from nature or everyday life.

Materials Needed

- ❒ white tagboard
- ❒ pattern
- ❒ scissors
- ❒ markers or crayons
- ❒ stickers (optional)

Directions

1. To make 40 shells of identical shape, trace the pattern on tagboard and cut out the pieces.
2. Use markers to decorate them, producing 20 identical pairs. *Optional:* To save time, you may use 20 pairs of stickers.

How to Play

1. Turn the shells design side down on a table.
2. Arrange them in three circles of 8, 13, and 18 shells (see diagram).
3. Place the remaining shell in the middle.
4. Each player turns over two shells, looking for a match. If a match is made, play continues. If not, the next player gets a turn.
5. The player with the most pairs is the winner.

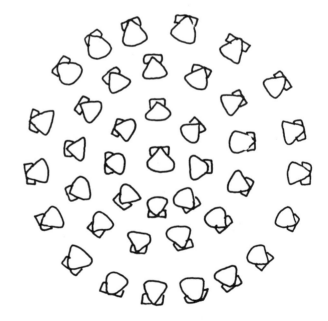

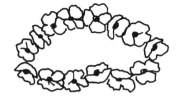

Lei

Lei are flower necklaces, given to people as they arrive or depart the Hawaiian Islands, or on other special occasions. They are usually made of plumeria blooms, although each island uses its own characteristic flower. As a hobby, Islanders often make lei from the flowers they grow in their gardens. The most expensive lei are made of small feathers or shells.

Materials Needed

- ❏ thin wire
- ❏ three packages of art tissue paper (different colors)
- ❏ scissors
- ❏ embroidery floss
- ❏ heavy needle

Directions

1. Cut the paper into 3" (76 mm) strips.
2. Open the strip and reroll it loosely.
3. Wire it together in the center.
4. Open the petals on either side of the wire.
5. Make lots of flowers.
6. Use the needle and several lengths of embroidery floss to sew through the flowers. Knot the ends of the floss.
7. You may want to make several lei to wear or give to your friends.

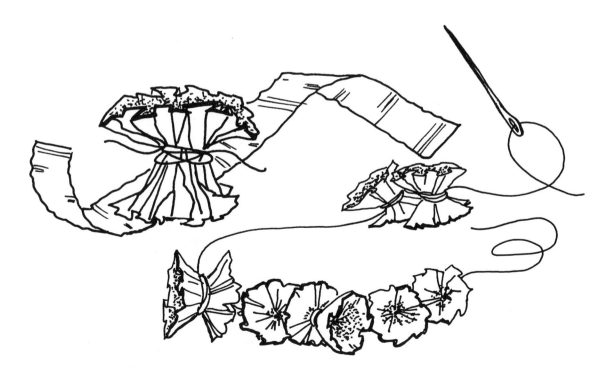

Nim

This game originated in ancient China and is still a favorite today. The game is played with 12 stones, placed in groupings of three, four, and five. The winner removes the last stone or groups. A variation of Nim allows you to play with any number of stones or game pieces.

Materials Needed

- ☐ 9" x 12" (229 x 305 mm) tagboard
- ☐ 39 game pieces (colored pasta shells)
- ☐ markers

Directions

1. Draw a game board on the tagboard (see diagram).
2. Use markers to decorate it.

How to Play

1. Place a game piece in each space on the game board.
2. The first player removes one, two, or three beans from any row. The second player does the same.
3. Players continue to alternate turns, never removing more than three game pieces at one time.
4. The object of the game is to force your opponent to pick up the last bean.

Origami Paper Crane

This traditional Japanese craft, handed down from parent to child, requires only a single sheet of paper.

Materials Needed

☐ 6" (152 mm) square of gift wrap or origami paper

Directions

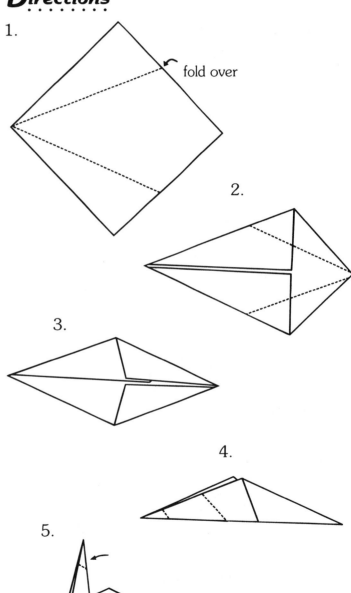

1.

fold over

2.

3.

4.

5.

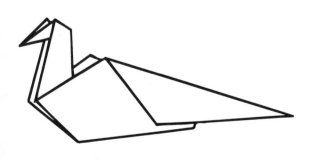

51

Paper Lantern

Teams of people work for weeks making lanterns for the springtime festival to honor Buddha's birthday. Crowds of people carry the lighted lanterns through the streets and leave them at the temple after making wishes.

Materials Needed

- ❑ 9" x 12" (229 x 305 mm) construction paper
- ❑ scissors
- ❑ glue
- ❑ markers or crayons
- ❑ string

Directions

1. Decorate your paper with markers or crayons.
2. Fold the paper in half lengthwise.
3. Make another fold about 1" (25 mm) from the outer edge (see diagram). Turn over the paper and repeat this step.
4. Make cuts at 1" (25 mm) intervals from the center fold to the outer folds.
5. Open the paper and glue the short ends together to make a cylinder.
6. Hang your lantern by a piece of string.
7. Refer to illustrations on the next page for other lanterns you might like to try.

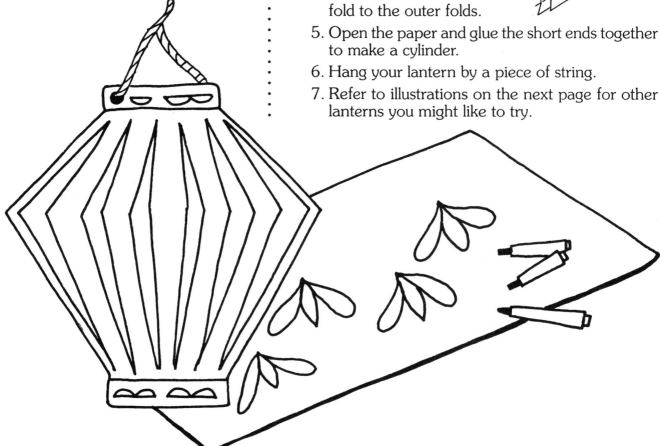

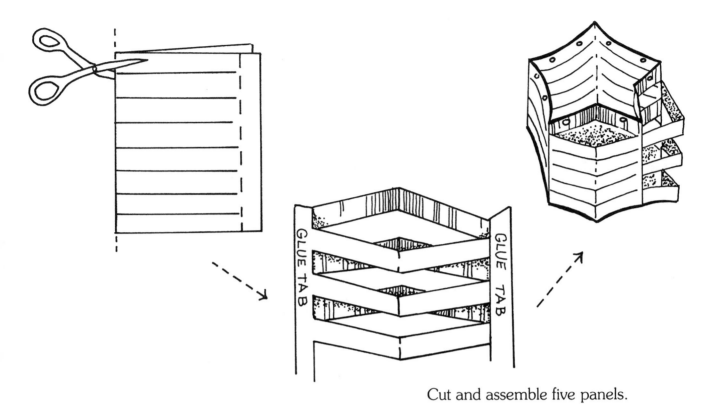

Cut and assemble five panels.

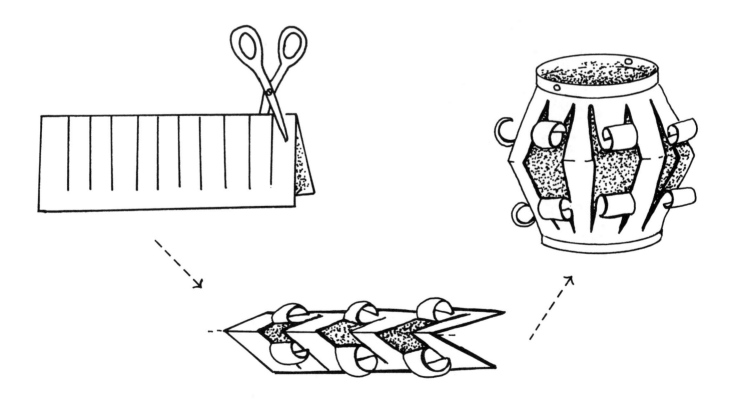

Tibet

Pellet Drum

These unusual drums are not struck with the hands or sticks. The two drum heads are struck by beads or pellets hanging from a string.

Materials Needed

- ❏ small plastic container with tight-fitting lid
- ❏ 12" x 1" (305 x 25 mm) dowel stick
- ❏ sharp scissors
- ❏ duct tape
- ❏ 12" (305 mm) length of cord
- ❏ two small beads (about ¾" or 19 mm in size)

Directions

1. Carefully pierce each side of the container. Insert the dowel through both holes.
2. Tear the duct tape to 1" (25 mm) width.
3. Wrap the tape tightly around the top end of the dowel to hold the container in place.
4. Wrap more tape around the dowel at the base of the container.
5. Tie the center of the cord around the stick under the container. Measure the length to the center of the container on each side and tie the beads securely place.

Prayer Mat

The rugs woven in the Middle East contain beautiful repeated geometric patterns. The rugs used in Muslim prayers have a center design that must face Mecca, Saudi Arabia.

Materials Needed

- ☐ 12" x 18" (305 x 457 mm) construction paper
- ☐ scissors
- ☐ pencil
- ☐ potato
- ☐ table knife
- ☐ ink pad
- ☐ ruler
- ☐ markers
- ☐ pictures of Islamic buildings and prayer rugs

Directions

1. Cut the potato in half. Draw a geometric design on the potato. Cut away the excess potato with the knife so that the design is raised about ½" (13 mm).

2. Use the scissors to fringe the two 12" (305 mm) sides of the paper.

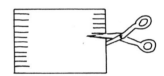

3. Use the ruler to measure a border inside the fringe.

4. Press the potato stamp onto the ink pad and decorate the border.

5. Use the markers to finish the center by drawing a geometric design.

Rakhi

During the festival of Raksha Bandhan, Hindu families renew their love for each other. A sister ties a braided bracelet (rakhi) on her brother's wrist. In return, he promises to always protect her.

Materials Needed

- □ several colors of yarn or narrow ribbon
- □ scissors
- □ colored tagboard scraps
- □ shiny materials (sequins, glitter, foil paper)
- □ glue
- □ heavy needle
- □ thread

Directions

1. Choose three colors of yarn or ribbon to make a 6"–7" (152–178 mm) braid.
2. Cut a small 1" (25 mm) circle from tagboard and decorate it with shiny materials.
3. Stitch the circle to the center of the bracelet.

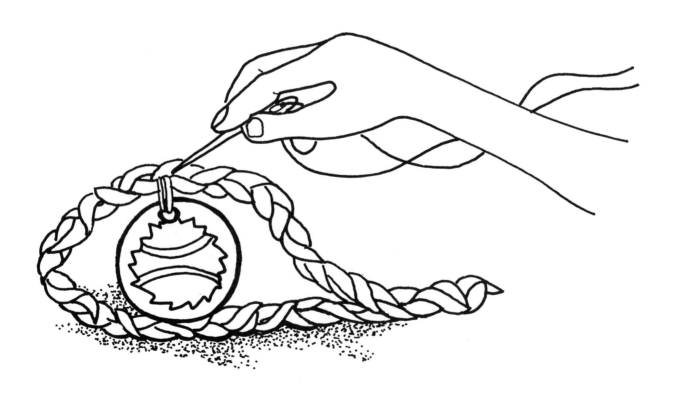

Shadow Puppet

These shadow puppets, known as *wayang kuhl*, are usually made from the skin of water buffalo. They are operated by a puppet master who also narrates the story. Performances begin in the middle of the night and end at sunrise. The audience may choose to watch the shadows from the front of the screen or move behind the screen to watch the puppeteer.

Materials Needed

- ❏ lightweight cardboard
- ❏ pencil
- ❏ sharp scissors
- ❏ paper fasteners
- ❏ hole punch
- ❏ masking tape
- ❏ two 10" (254 mm) pieces of coat hanger wire
- ❏ pattern on page 58

Directions

1. Enlarge the pattern and cut out pieces from cardboard. Use the sharp scissors to cut around the details.
2. Punch a hole at each "X."
3. Join the arms and legs with paper fasteners.
4. Tape one of the wires to each arm, or one to an arm and the other to the body. (You may wish to tape wires to the arms and body, and have two children operate one puppet.)

How to Use

1. Show your puppets on a white sheet hung in a darkened classroom.
2. Shine a bright light from a lamp or filmstrip projector onto one side of the white surface.
3. Hold the puppets between the light and the screen.

Shisha Mirror Vest

Shishadur is the ancient East Indian art of stitching mirrors to cloth. It is used for wall hangings, rugs, and clothing decorations.

Materials Needed

- ☐ large paper grocery bag
- ☐ bowl of water
- ☐ red tempera paint
- ☐ sponge
- ☐ scissors
- ☐ aluminum foil
- ☐ glue
- ☐ markers or crayons

Directions

1. Soak the bag in water for a few minutes,
2. Squeeze out the excess water from the paper, and allow it to dry about twenty minutes.
3. Sponge paint the bag.
4. Flatten the bag and let it dry thoroughly.
5. Crease the bottom of the bag through the center, and cut out the neckline and arm holes. Cut through the center front.
6. Shape the bottom of the vest as desired.
7. Cut out several small holes on the front of your vest. Glue foil **behind** the holes.
8. Design "embroidery" with markers on the front of the vest.
9. Decorate the back of the vest in the same manner.

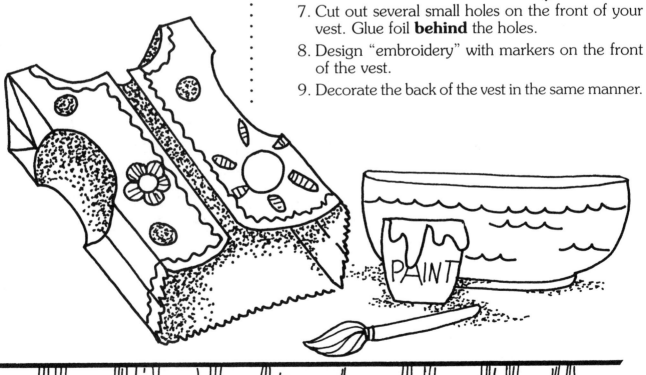

Spoon Doll

This doll is wearing the traditional kimono of Japan.

Materials Needed

- ❏ wooden kitchen spoon
- ❏ black yarn
- ❏ wallpaper samples
- ❏ tan construction paper scraps
- ❏ scissors
- ❏ glue
- ❏ black marker

Directions

1. Draw a face on the spoon with markers. Cut the yarn hair and glue in place.

2. Cut two identical kimonos from wallpaper. These will be the front and back of the body.

3. Cut two hands and feet from the tan construction paper.

4. Glue the hands and feet in place on the inside of the back kimono.

5. Glue the spoon handle (face forward) through the center of that kimono.

6. Finish the doll by gluing the top kimono in place around the edges.

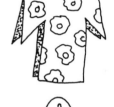

Stamping Stick

These percussion instruments provide a strong beat for dancing. The hollow sticks are banged against the ground and sound echoes into the tube.

Materials Needed

- ❑ several large tubes of different sizes (wrapping paper or mailing tubes)
- ❑ cardboard
- ❑ masking tape
- ❑ brightly colored paints
- ❑ paintbrushes
- ❑ buttons and string, chains to vary the sound
- ❑ sharp scissors

Directions

1. Decorate the tubes with colorful designs.
2. Poke holes and add chains or buttons on strings to the tubes as shown.
3. Cut a circle from cardboard about 2" (51 mm) larger in diameter than the end of the tube.
4. To cover one end of the tube, cut notches in the circle. Fold the cardboard as shown, and tape it in place at the end of the tube.

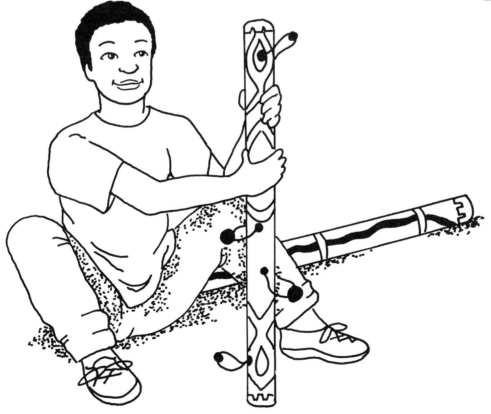

Tangrams

The Chinese call this familiar puzzle a Qi-Qiao Ban (chee chee ow bahn). These are geometric shapes which can be used to make many pictures.

Materials Needed

☐ 8" (203 mm) square paper
☐ scissors

1.

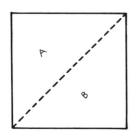

2.

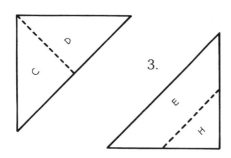

3.

4.

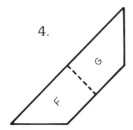

5.

6.

Directions

1. Fold the square in half to make two triangles (A and B). Make a sharp crease and then cut apart the triangles on the fold.

2. Fold triangle A in half to make two smaller-sized triangles (C and D). Make a sharp crease and cut apart the triangles on the fold. Set triangles C and D aside.

3. Fold triangle B to make two pieces by aligning the point of triangle with the longest edge (see diagram). Make a sharp crease and cut apart the pieces (triangle H and trapezoid E). Set aside triangle H.

4. Fold the trapezoid in half. Cut apart the pieces F and G.

5. Take piece F and align the top corner with the lower edge. Make a sharp crease (see diagram) and cut apart the pieces (triangle and parallelogram). Set aside the pieces.

6. Take piece G and fold it in half (see diagram). Make a sharp crease and cut apart the pieces (square and triangle).

How To Use

1. Use your seven tans to make various figures (man, cat, dog, bird, woman, and others.)

2. Remember that all seven tans must be used and no edges can overlap.

Wind Chimes

Wind chimes were originally made to hang in the temples of the Far East. They create a light, pleasant, tinkling sound when they are moved by the wind.

Materials Needed

- ❏ heavy cardboard
- ❏ hole punch
- ❏ sharp scissors
- ❏ string or yarn
- ❏ two empty spools from thread
- ❏ glue
- ❏ decorative braid, fringe, or rickrack
- ❏ assorted bells
- ❏ tube pasta
- ❏ wooden beads
- ❏ tempera paint
- ❏ small paintbrushes

Directions

1. Cut out a circle about 8" (203 mm) in diameter from cardboard.
2. Paint a design on the circle. Allow the paint to dry.
3. Glue decorative braid around the outer edge of the circle.
4. Punch eight holes around the circumference of the circle and one in the center.
5. Cut eight strings of different lengths.
6. Thread one string through each hole and knot one end to hold it in place.
7. Thread a variety of pasta, bells, and beads on each string and then make a large knot to hold the items on the string.
8. To make a hanger, tie one spool securely to the end of an 18" (457 mm) length of string and poke the string up through the center hole. Feed the string through the second spool and glue it firmly to the top of the cardboard circle.
9. Make a hanging loop.

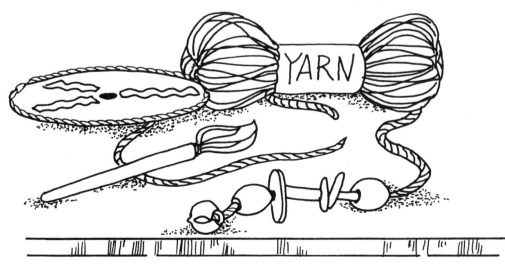

EUROPE

Bilboquet . . . .

King Henri III of France enjoyed this children's game during the late 1500s. His interest was shared by members of his court and the French people. Early bilboquet cups were carved from wood and painted with designs.

Materials Needed

☐ large wooden bead
☐ Styrofoam cup
☐ 18" (457 mm) piece of string
☐ scissors
☐ markers or paint

Directions

1. Decorate your cup with markers.
2. Use the scissors to poke a small hole in the bottom of the cup. Thread the string through the hole and knot it securely.
3. Thread the other end of the string through the bead and knot it securely.

To Play

1. Hold the cup in your hand letting the ball hang freely.
2. Move the cup to cause the ball to fly up and then catch the ball in the cup.

Castle

Thousands of castles were built throughout Europe during the Middle Ages. They were really forts, built on cliffs, coastlines, or rivers, to protect the owners and their lands and families. Because the castles were built close to neighboring villages, they often served as local prisons and courthouses.

Materials Needed

- [ ] 8 small cardboard boxes, similar in height
- [ ] corrugated cardboard
- [ ] lightweight cardboard
- [ ] masking tape
- [ ] glue
- [ ] pencil
- [ ] scissors, X-acto knife
- [ ] ruler
- [ ] paint

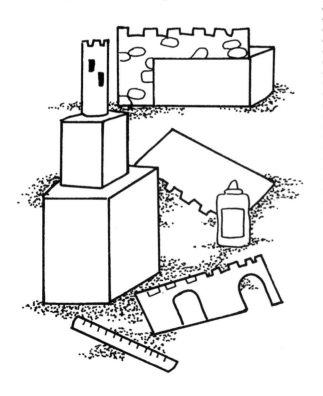

Directions

Gatehouse:

1. Determine the height of the gatehouse.
2. Use that height when cutting a rectangular piece of corrugated cardboard.
3. Divide the rectangle into fourths and score down the sides.

4. Cut notches along the top edge and a door in the bottom front of the second section. Use the cutout door piece as a pattern when cutting a second door in the fourth section.

5. Fold the cardboard and tape securely down the open edge.
6. If the castle will have a moat, design a drawbridge that is long enough to cross it. Attach the drawbridge in front of the door.

Towers:

1. Determine the height of the towers.
2. Use that height when cutting a rectangular piece of lightweight cardboard.
3. Cut notches along the top edge of the rectangle and cut out the windows.
4. Roll the cardboard into a tube and tape it securely.
5. Repeat steps to make five additional towers.

To Finish the Castle:

1. Arrange your boxes into a four-sided figure, two on each side.

2. Connect them with towers at the corners.

3. Place the gatehouse at the center of the **front** wall with a tower on each side (see diagram).

4. Cut notched outer walls from cardboard to fit over the boxes.

5. Glue the walls in place.

6. Connect all pieces with masking tape on the **inside**.

7. Paint the castle gray (stone) or brown (wood).

8. Set your castle on green paper and design a center courtyard. Place a blue paper moat along the outer edge of the castle walls.

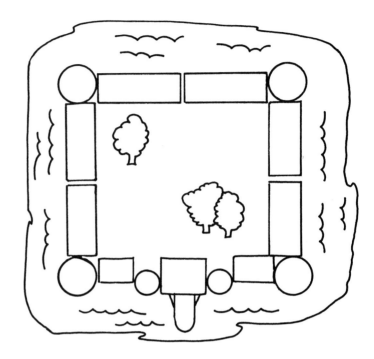

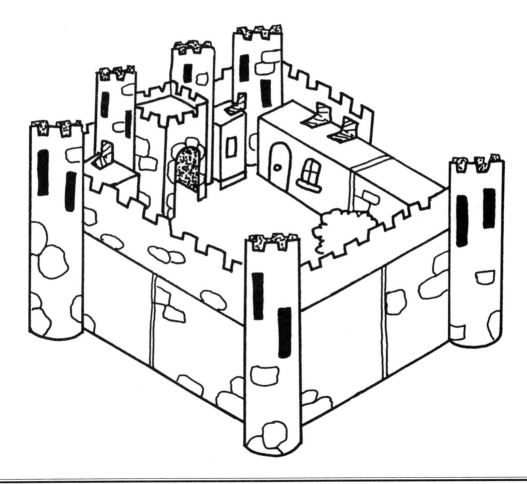

Christmas Cracker

These colorful little gifts are used as party favors during English holiday celebrations. Two people pull the cracker apart, and the one who gets the longest end keeps the gift.

Materials Needed

- ☐ cardboard tubes (from paper towels)
- ☐ small toys or gifts (that will fit inside the tubes)
- ☐ shiny gift-wrap paper (several colors)
- ☐ tissue paper
- ☐ stars, stickers for decorations
- ☐ narrow ribbon or yarn
- ☐ scissors
- ☐ transparent tape
- ☐ glue

Directions

1. Cut the cardboard tube into two uneven pieces.
2. Insert one part of the tube inside the other.
3. Put the toy inside the tube and stuff the ends with tissue paper.
4. Cut a piece of gift wrap twice as long as the tube. Fringe the ends or cut in a zigzag shape.
5. Roll the paper around the tube. Tape in place.
6. Twist the ends closed. Tie with ribbon or yarn.
7. Decorate the package with stars or stickers, or glue on paper shapes cut from gift wrap.

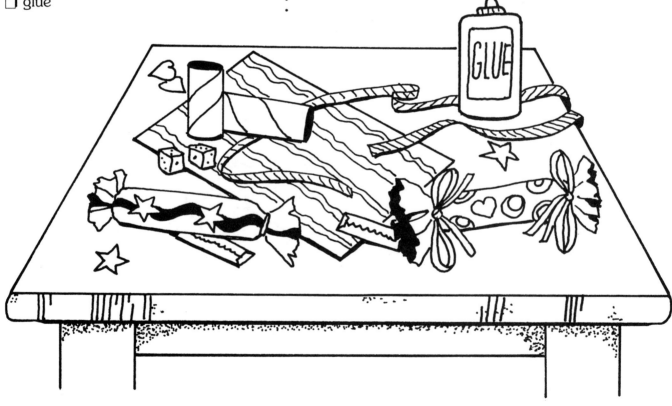

Cowbell

In Switzerland and Austria, the cows graze on the mountainsides. The gentle tinkling of their bells lets farmers know their location.

Materials Needed

- ☐ clay flowerpot, 3" (76 mm) diameter
- ☐ small bell
- ☐ ribbon
- ☐ small ball of clay
- ☐ paints

Directions

1. Paint decorations on the flowerpot. Allow to dry.
2. Thread the ribbon through the bell and then through the hole in the pot.
3. Apply a ball of clay **inside** the pot at the hole to keep the bell swinging freely.
4. Tie the ends of the ribbon in a bow.

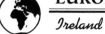

Crois Bride

The farmers of Ireland celebrate the feast day of St. Brigid, the patron saint of dairy cows, by decorating their barns with these simple crosses, crois bride (cris breedge). They believe the crosses will protect their barns from fire and their cattle from harm.

Materials Needed

☐ tall, dry grass
   (about 12" or 305 mm)
☐ string or yarn
☐ scissors

Directions

1. Divide the grass into two even bunches and tie yarn around one end of each bunch.

2. Separate each bunch into three parts. Weave two parts under and one over as shown below.

3. Tie the finished ends together and hang the cross on your door.

Dissected Puzzles

The first puzzles were made in England in the 1800s. They were called "dissected" puzzles, because they were cut into pieces. Pictures of battles and maps were painted on thin boards and made into puzzles so that children could use them to learn about history.

Materials Needed

- ☐ old calendar pictures
- ☐ white glue
- ☐ 1" (25 mm) paintbrush
- ☐ tagboard
- ☐ sharp scissors or utility knife

Directions

1. Apply a thin layer of glue to the back of the picture. Allow it to dry.
2. Cut a piece of tagboard the same size as the picture. Apply a thin layer of glue to the back of the tagboard.

3. While it is still wet, line up the edges of the picture with the tagboard and press the glued sides together.
4. Cut the picture into puzzle pieces after the wet mounting has dried.

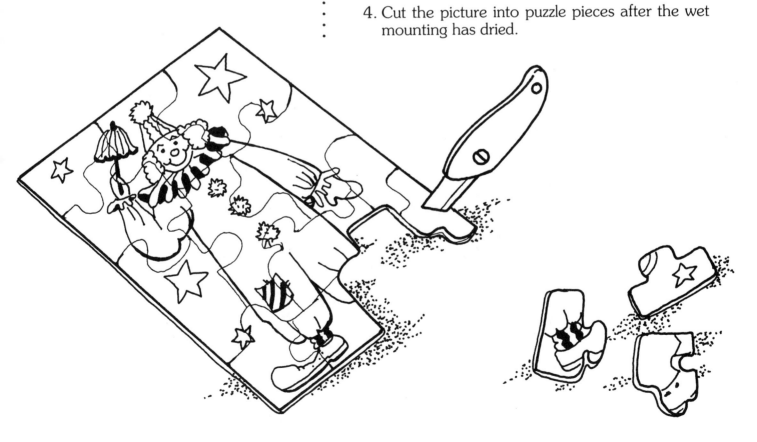

Family Crest

Families around the world design crests to express the meaning of their names, their work, or the importance of their positions. Each of the Highland clans people of Scotland have special tartans (plaid patterns) that date back to the 1700s.

Materials Needed

- ☐ 9" x 12" (229 x 305) white construction paper
- ☐ 12" x 18" (305 x 457 mm) colored construction paper
- ☐ ruler
- ☐ pencil
- ☐ markers or crayons
- ☐ scissors
- ☐ glue

Directions

1. Look at several examples of tartans before you begin. Point out the repeated pattern in the plaid. Decide on a plaid to copy or choose three colors and design your own.
2. Draw the outline of the crest on the white construction paper.
3. Divide the crest into sections. (See diagram.)
4. Draw the plaid in the bottom section of the crest.
5. Neatly print your last name through the center section.
6. Fill the top sections with drawings of things that are important to you and your family.
7. Cut out your crest and glue it to colored construction paper.

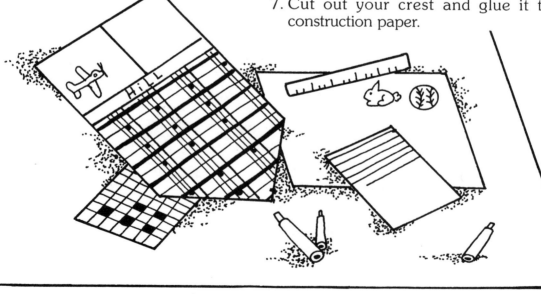

Greek Vase

The pictures and patterns on Greek vases showed how the people lived 2,500 years ago. The vases were made in different shapes, either for drinking, or for storing wine or oil. The single-handled, narrow-necked *lekythos* held oil, while the large *amphora* vase which had two handles, held wine or oil.

Materials Needed

- ☐ plastic bottle
- ☐ clay (terra-cotta color)
- ☐ sharp scissors
- ☐ pipe cleaners
- ☐ black paint
- ☐ fine paintbrushes
- ☐ pictures of Greek vases

Directions

1. Twist several pipe cleaners together to make a strong wire.
2. Poke holes in the bottle for the handle(s) and insert the pipe cleaners.
3. Cover the entire bottle (including handles) with clay. Apply a little extra at the joints of the bottle and handles.
4. Make all the clay as smooth as possible. Allow it to dry.
5. Study Greek designs and paint one on your vase.

Greeting Cards

The first Christmas card was printed in England in 1843. Some people believe that the earliest cards were Valentines sent to sweethearts in the 1700s. The early Christmas cards were colored by hand and sold for as much as a day's wages, and the Victorian Valentine was decorated with lace and ribbons.

Materials Needed

- ☐ heavy paper or tagboard (10" x 6" or 254 x 152 mm)
- ☐ small doily
- ☐ lace scraps
- ☐ ribbons
- ☐ glue
- ☐ floral printed gift wrap
- ☐ scissors
- ☐ marker or pen

Directions

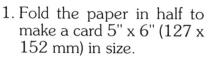

1. Fold the paper in half to make a card 5" x 6" (127 x 152 mm) in size.
2. Cut out some flowers. Select pieces of lace and ribbons, and a doily.
3. Arrange the items on the front of the card to make a pretty design.
4. Glue them in place.
5. Write a verse on the inside of the card.
6. Send it to a friend or family member.

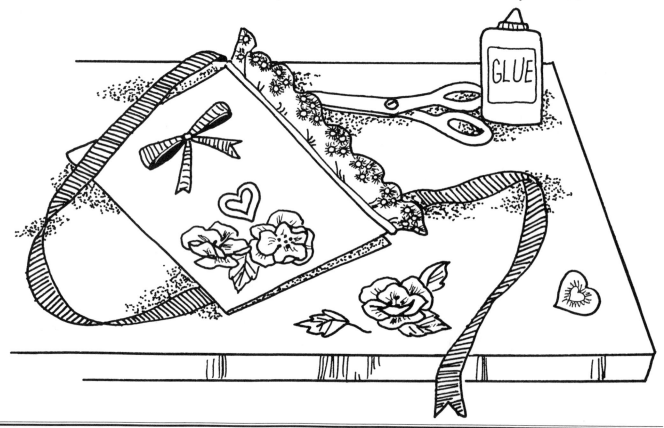

Illuminated Manuscript

During the Middle Ages scribes spent their entire lives making copies of existing texts. Many of the manuscripts were religious in nature. The illuminators added many beautiful decorations to their hand-lettered writings.

Materials Needed

- ☐ letter patterns on page 76
- ☐ white writing paper
- ☐ colored pencils or watercolors
- ☐ pen or marker

Directions

1. Carefully write your favorite verse or poem.
2. Begin some of the lines with letters cut from the illuminated manuscript. Add your own decorations.
3. Color the lettering and decorations with colored pencils or watercolor paints.

Little Boy Blue, come blow your horn! The sheep's in the meadow, the cow's in the corn. Where's the little boy that looks after the sheep? Under the haystack, fast asleep!

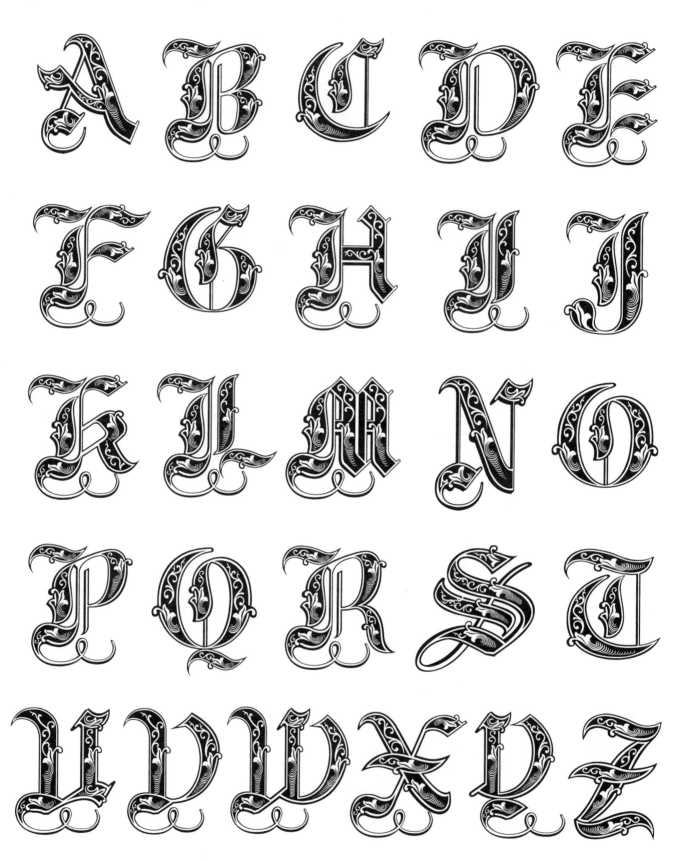

Juleneg

Danish farmers traditionally put out bundles of oats to feed the birds. They believe that the juleneg has magic to protect the next season's crops from being eaten.

Materials Needed

- ☐ ½ gallon (1.89L) milk container (paper or plastic)
- ☐ two small sturdy boxes
- ☐ scissors
- ☐ stapler
- ☐ wire
- ☐ wire cutters
- ☐ birdseed, nuts, suet, popcorn, dried fruit

Directions

1. Cut openings on two sides of the container.
2. Staple the small boxes under the openings for perches.
3. Poke holes through the top and insert the wire. Twist the wire to a loop for hanging.
4. Fill the feeder with food for the birds. Hang it where you can watch them feeding.

Majstång

The coming of summer is very important in the Scandinavian countries. In many Swedish villages it is marked by the appearance of the maypole (majstång) on the village green.

Materials Needed

- [ ] two fairly large, straight sticks
- [ ] wire
- [ ] string
- [ ] yarn
- [ ] ribbon
- [ ] brightly colored paper scraps
- [ ] scissors
- [ ] glue or transparent tape

Directions

1. Use the wire to bind the sticks together in the shape of a cross.
2. Create a long vine of flowers and leaves from the paper scraps, string and tape.
3. Wrap the vine around the sticks.
4. Fill in the empty spaces with bits of colored yarn and ribbons.

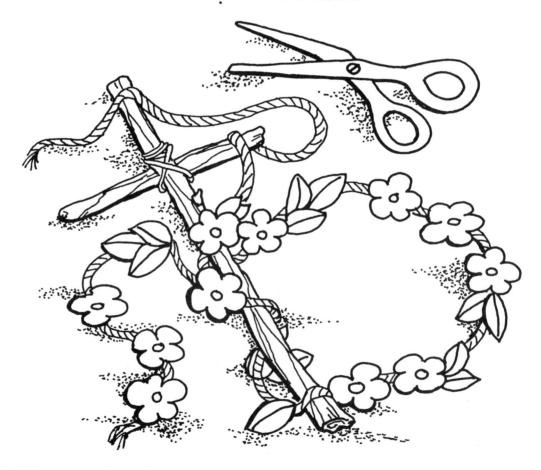

Mardi Gras Mask

The Mardi Gras celebration is held on Shrove Tuesday, the day before the start of Lent. Mardi Gras means *fat Tuesday* in French. It is celebrated in Nice, France, with a colorful parade through town. French colonists introduced Mardi Gras to the United States in the early 1700s.

Materials Needed

- ❏ paper plate, or colored tagboard, 8" x 10" (203 x 254 mm)
- ❏ craft stick
- ❏ scissors
- ❏ glue
- ❏ markers or crayons
- ❏ craft materials (feathers, beads, sequins, glitter, ribbon)

Directions

1. Cut out a mask from the paper plate or tagboard. (See diagram.) Carefully cut out the eye holes.
2. Use the feathers, beads, other craft materials, and markers to decorate the mask.

3. Glue the craft stick to the back of the mask to make a handle.

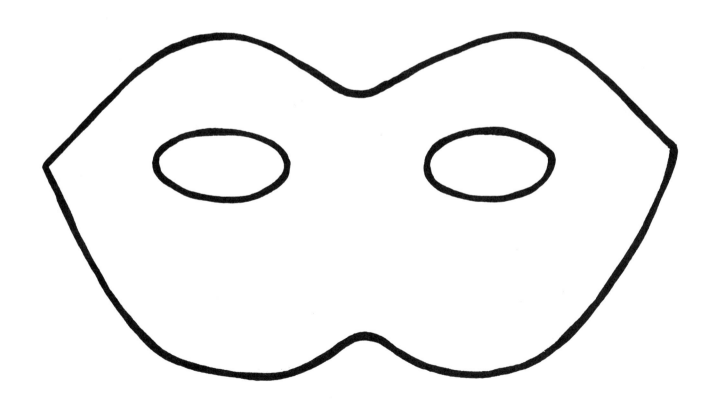

Maundy Purse

On the Thursday before Easter the Queen of England gives purses holding special coins to old men and women at a Maundy ceremony. The word "Maundy" comes from the Latin meaning commandment.

Materials Needed

- ☐ brightly colored felt
- ☐ needle and thread
- ☐ scissors
- ☐ X-acto knife
- ☐ pinking shears
- ☐ ½" (13 mm) wide ribbon
- ☐ tagboard scraps
- ☐ school glue
- ☐ foil scraps

Directions

Purse:

1. Cut the felt into two identical pieces about 4" x 6" (102 x 152 mm).
2. Round the corners.
3. Stitch around three sides of the purse. Make strong knots at the start and finish.
4. Cut across the top with pinking shears.
5. Ask an adult to help you use the X-acto knife to cut slits about an inch (25 mm) under the pinked edge.
6. Weave the ribbon in and out of the slits.
7. Pull the ribbon to close the purse, and then tie a bow.

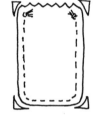

Coins:

1. Cut the tagboard into several small circles.
2. Make a design with glue on each circle. Set them aside to dry completely.
3. Cover the coins with aluminum foil. Smooth the foil so that the relief of the glue design will show.

Mosaic

Miniature mosaics are made by skilled craftsmen who use small pieces of colored glass and silver to create beautiful jewelry.

Materials Needed

- [ ] eggshells, cleaned and dried
- [ ] tempera paints (three or more colors)
- [ ] school glue (dries clear)
- [ ] cardboard
- [ ] aluminum foil
- [ ] scissors and hole punch
- [ ] tweezers
- [ ] gold or silver cord
- [ ] clear nail polish (optional)
- [ ] pencil
- [ ] small paintbrush

Directions

1. Wash the eggshells in soapy water, peeling off the inner membrane. Do not break the eggshells. Allow them to dry overnight.
2. Paint the inside and outside of the shells different colors. Allow them to dry.
3. Crush shells into small pieces, keeping the different colors separated.
4. Cut a small oval or circle from cardboard. Cover it with aluminum foil. Mark a simple design for your mosaic on the foil.

5. Spread glue on **one** section and press the eggshells into place. Use a tweezer if needed. Continue until the pendant is covered, leaving a small open space near the top.
6. Punch a hole at the top of the pendant.
7. Coat the mosaic with clear nail polish if desired.
8. Attach a length of cord.

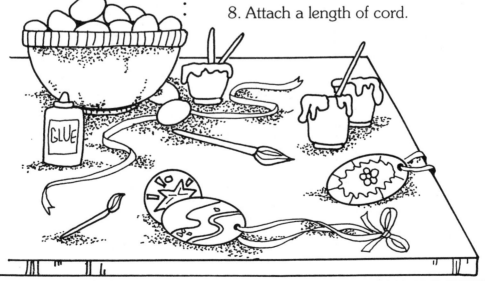

Nesting Dolls

Nesting dolls are made of wood with painted faces and decoration. These sets of different-sized dolls, also known as *matryoshka* sets, are a popular toy of Russian children. Because grandmothers use the dolls to entertain their grandchildren, the toy was named after them. Most sets have five or six dolls, however some sets have as many as fifteen dolls.

Materials Needed

- ☐ cardboard tube (toilet tissue)
- ☐ lightweight cardboard, 5" x 7" (127 x 178 mm) rectangle
- ☐ lightweight cardboard, 6" x 8½" (152 x 216 mm) rectangle
- ☐ pattern on page 83
- ☐ crayons or markers
- ☐ glue
- ☐ transparent tape or stapler
- ☐ scissors

Directions

1. Make three different-sized patterns. Photocopy the pattern at 120%, 100%, and 78%.
2. Color and cut out the three patterns.
3. Glue the smallest pattern to the toilet tissue tube.
4. Glue the middle-sized and largest patterns to the pieces of lightweight cardboard
5. Roll the patterns into cylinders, overlapping the edges about ½" (13 mm). Tape or staple the edges together.

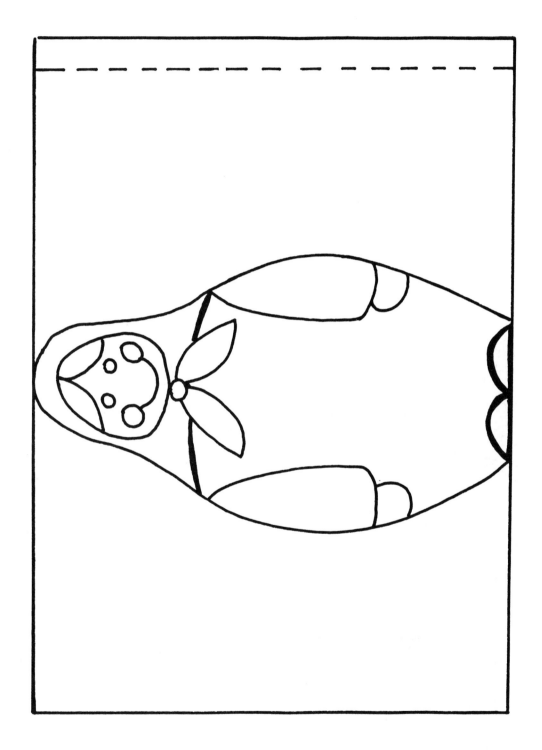

Paper Filigree

This popular craft from the 18th century is now known as quilling. The method can be used to create a picture or embellish an existing one.

Materials Needed

- ☐ colored paper strips, ⅛" (3 mm) width
- ☐ white glue (dries clear)
- ☐ black tagboard, 8" x 10" (203 x 254 mm) in size
- ☐ toothpicks
- ☐ 6" (152 mm) length of black ribbon

Directions

1. If you wish to embellish a favorite picture (or poem), glue it to the black cardboard. If not, you can create a picture to fill the background.

2. *Preparation:* Cut paper strips with a paper cutter.

3. Experiment with rolling the paper strips around toothpicks and pinching them to make a variety of coil shapes (see diagram).

4. Hold the shapes together with a dab of glue.

5. Combine several shapes and glue them to the cardboard.

6. Attach a black ribbon loop at the top for a hanger.

Paper Cuts

Creating works of art with paper still fascinates people today. The intricately cut paper designs made in Poland are known as *wycinanki* (ve che non' ke). These fine symmetrical designs in dark colored paper are either circular (called stars) or rectangular shaped, some having layers of colorful pieces added to enhance the designs. Traditional paper cuts feature the spruce tree, human figure, floral, birds, or rooster motifs. The heart design is a traditional motif of the German *scherenschnitte* (sher en shnit' uh). In Germany, bakers use paper doilies when decorating cakes by sprinkling powder sugar through the intricate paper designs.

Materials Needed

- ❏ lightweight colored paper
- ❏ pencil
- ❏ small sharp scissors (embroidery scissors)
- ❏ hole punch
- ❏ glue
- ❏ black tagboard or construction paper

Directions

Paper Doily:

1. For the paper doily, begin with a circle of paper. Fold the paper in half three time.

2. Cut an interesting edging for your doily.

3. Follow the illustration as you cut out the heart and tulip designs.

4. Open the doily carefully and flatten it between heavy books.

5. Create your own paper doilies.

Star Paper Cut:

Patterns:

1. For a star design that has layers of colored paper, select lightweight black paper. Cut the paper into a 10" (254 mm) circular shape.

2. Fold the paper three times in half.

3. Use the flower pattern and cut out the flower design. Make a wide cut around each flower to highlight them.

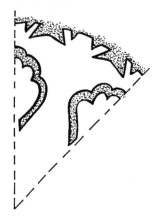

3. Open the folded paper twice and transfer the bird pattern to your design. Make a wide cut around the bird to highlight it. (See illustration below.)

4. Open the star design carefully. Choose two or three different colors for decorating the flowers and the birds. First cut out the flower shapes that fit inside the flowers (see below) and glue them in place. Using the patterns for the bird's wing, cut out each wing piece from different colored paper and glue them in place (see below). Repeat this step for decorating the other bird in the design.

5. If you prefer, add additional layers of colors to your star design.

St. Lucia Crown

Saint Lucia's Day is celebrated in several European countries. In Sweden, she is the patron saint of light. Each town has a Lucia queen. On December 13 she walks through town in a long white dress wearing a crown of candles. Her attendants are clad in white garments—either wearing tinsel in their hair (girls) or tall paper cones that are decorated with stars (boys).

Materials Needed

- ☐ white tagboard
- ☐ stapler
- ☐ four 6" (152 mm) cardboard tubes
- ☐ white paint
- ☐ paintbrush
- ☐ scissors
- ☐ yellow and orange tissue paper scraps
- ☐ glue
- ☐ masking tape
- ☐ silver tinsel or artificial evergreens

Directions

1. Cut a strip of white tagboard 2½" (64 mm) wide and long enough to wrap around your head with a 1" (25 mm) overlap. Staple it to make a headband.
2. Paint the tubes white and allow to dry.
3. Cut tissue paper flames and glue them in the candles.
4. Cut 2" (51 mm) slits on each side at the base of the tubes.
5. Fit them down onto the tagboard headband. If necessary, tape the candles in place from the inside.
6. Staple tinsel decorations or artificial evergreens on the headband.

Schultüte

Children entering the first grade in German schools are given a *schultüte* by their parents. The small gifts and supplies make the first day of school more special.

Materials Needed

- ❏ 9" x 12" or (229 x 305 mm) construction paper
- ❏ tissue paper
- ❏ scissors
- ❏ glue or transparent tape
- ❏ markers
- ❏ gifts (candies, gum, balloons, pencils, erasers, stickers)
- ❏ 15" (381 mm) piece of ribbon or yarn

Directions

1. Fold the construction paper in half and cut as shown.
2. Unfold and decorate the paper with markers.
3. Slightly pleat a 6" (152 mm) wide strip of tissue paper and glue it to the **rounded** edge of the construction paper.
4. Shape the construction paper into a cone and secure the side with glue or tape. Do **not** glue or tape the tissue.
5. Fill the cone with small gifts and tie the tissue paper closed with a ribbon.

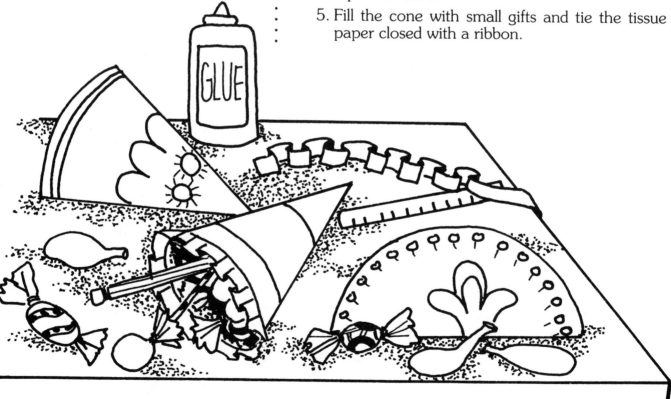

Stained Glass

Stained glass decorates the cathedral windows of England. Pieces of glass are cut and painted, then soldered together with lead. The large windows are made in small sections and fit into an iron framework. Many of the windows tell stories or honor historical or religious figures.

Materials Needed

- ❏ pattern
- ❏ gallon-size (3.79L) heavy-duty resealable plastic bag
- ❏ cardboard
- ❏ scissors
- ❏ black electrical tape
- ❏ permanent felt-tipped markers

Directions

1. Cut the cardboard to fit into the plastic bag.
2. Place the cardboard and picture pattern inside the bag. Close the bag.
3. Lay strips of tape on the plastic to outline the picture.

4. Fill in the taped sections with colored markers.
5. Remove the cardboard and picture. Flatten and seal the bag.
6. Hang your stained glass in a sunny window.

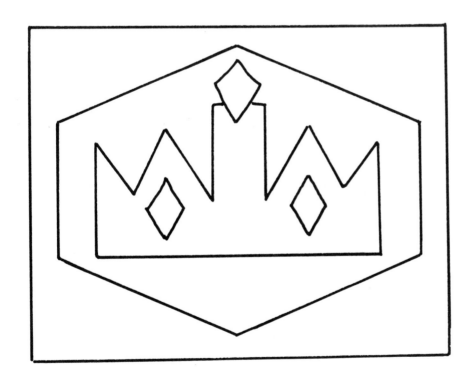

Ukrainian Eggs

Ukrainian Easter eggs, called *pysanky,* are decorated with a wax resist technique. They are among the most beautiful and valuable in the world.

Materials Needed

- ❐ hard-boiled eggs
- ❐ egg coloring kit (cold water type) or prepare natural dyes with onion skins, beet juice, etc.
- ❐ paraffin
- ❐ double boiler
- ❐ thin paintbrush

Directions

CAUTION: Have an adult melt the paraffin in the double boiler.

1. Dip the paintbrush into the wax and paint designs onto clean, cool eggs. Be sure the design is balanced geometrically.

2. Allow the wax to dry.

3. Dye the eggs according to package directions.

4. *Note:* If you wish to use two dye colors, add a second layer of wax to the egg before dipping it in a second dye color. Dye lighter colors first and darker, more opaque colors second.

Windmill

Windmills were popular toys in Europe as early as the 1500s. They represented the windmills of the Netherlands that pump water from land which lies below sea level.

Materials Needed

- ❏ lightweight tagboard, 8" (203 mm) square
- ❏ ruler
- ❏ scissors
- ❏ paper fastener
- ❏ hole punch
- ❏ cardboard tube (paper towel) or large, plastic, drinking straw
- ❏ paint or markers

Directions

1. Draw or paint designs of one side of the tagboard.
2. Divide the unpainted side into fourths (from corner to corner as shown) with a ruler. Mark the center point.
3. Cut along the four lines, leaving the tagboard joined at the center.

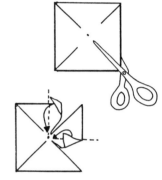

4. Fold one corner of each sail towards the center, making sure the flaps overlap.
5. Put the fastener through the sails and the center mark.
6. Decorate the cardboard tube.
7. Punch a hole in the tube for the sails. If you use a straw, flatten it and punch a hole.
8. Attach the sails loosely to the cardboard tube (or straw) with the paper fastener enabling the windmill to rotate when the wind hits it.

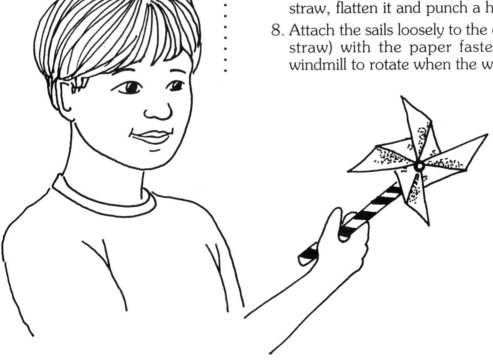

Woven Heart

It is believed that Hans Christian Anderson may have invented the famous Danish woven heart. It is made in the colors of the national flag. During past wartimes it was displayed as a silent symbol of patriotism.

Materials Needed

- ❏ red and white construction paper, 4" x 12" (102 x 305 mm) in size
- ❏ scissors
- ❏ glue
- ❏ construction paper strip (red or white)

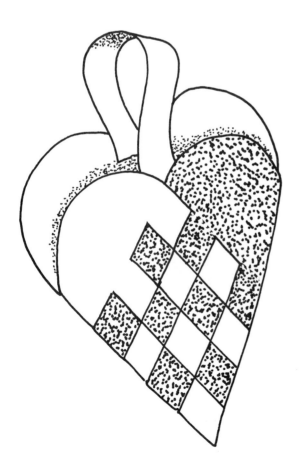

Directions

1. Fold the red and white papers in half lengthwise.

2. Cut the paper to round the edges as shown. Be sure you are **not** trimming the folded edges. Cut three slits.

3. Place the folded papers side by side on the table with the rounded edges facing you, white paper on the right side.

4. To weave, begin with the first loop of the white half of the heart. Insert the white loop into the first red loop. Open the white loop to insert the next red loop. Continue until the first row is finished.

5. For the second row, turn the heart over and begin with the top red loop. Continue as with the first row.

6. Repeat until the whole heart is woven. *Note:* Be careful not to tear the last row.

7. Glue a strip of construcion paper to the top for a handle.

NORTH & SOUTH AMERICA

Adobe House

The early people that lived in the American Southwest built fascinating adobe structures—such as the Mesa Verde dwellings. In some settlements, the houses were three stories tall. These Native people used ladders to reach the entrances on the roofs. Today, the Pueblo people still make their one-story houses with sun-baked adobe bricks. The thick walls keep the houses cool in the hot sunshine.

Materials Needed

- ☐ two or three small cardboard boxes in graduated sizes
- ☐ clay (terra-cotta color)
- ☐ utility knife or sharp scissors
- ☐ long twigs and sticks
- ☐ wire

Directions

1. Turn the boxes upside down. (The box bottom will become the roof line). Cut several windows in each box. In the smallest box, cut a small opening in the roof.

2. Cover the sides of the boxes with clay. Make the clay as smooth as possible.

3. Stack the boxes with the largest on the bottom.

4. Spread twigs on the roofs and cover them with clay. Allow the ends of the twigs to show. (In an adobe house, beams are used to support the weight of the roof.)

Optional: Design a ladder from sticks. Use thin wire to bind the steps in place.

*A*nimalito

These little stuffed toys are made by weaving cotton in brightly-colored stripes. Used as toys or decorations, they may be shaped like dogs, rabbits, birds, or donkeys.

*M*aterials *N*eeded

- ❐ two 9" (229 mm) squares of heavy white paper or wrapping paper scraps
- ❐ cotton balls or tissue (for stuffing)
- ❐ white glue
- ❐ markers or crayons
- ❐ scissors
- ❐ yarn scraps
- ❐ patterns on pages 96 and 97

*D*irections

1. Choose one of the suggested shapes shown below. Enlarge the shape when making a photocopy of it. Cut out one shape for the front of your animal.

2. Glue the animal around the edge to the other piece of paper, leaving an opening as shown. When the glue is dry, cut away the excess paper.

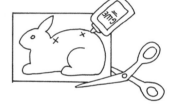

3. If you have used plain paper, decorate the front and back with matching stripes.

4. Stuff the animal with cotton at the opening.

5. Punch a hole for a yarn hanger as shown. Insert a tail in the opening and secure it by glueing.

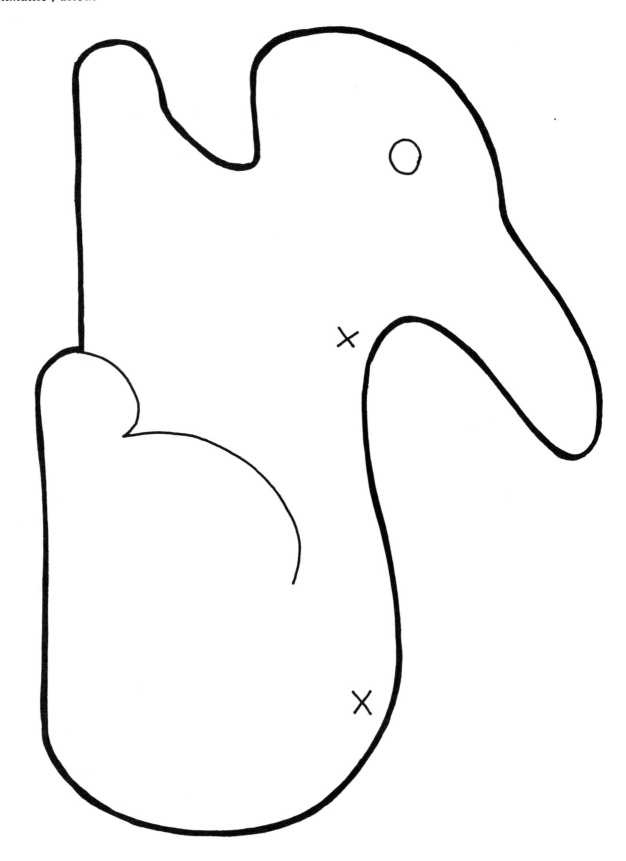

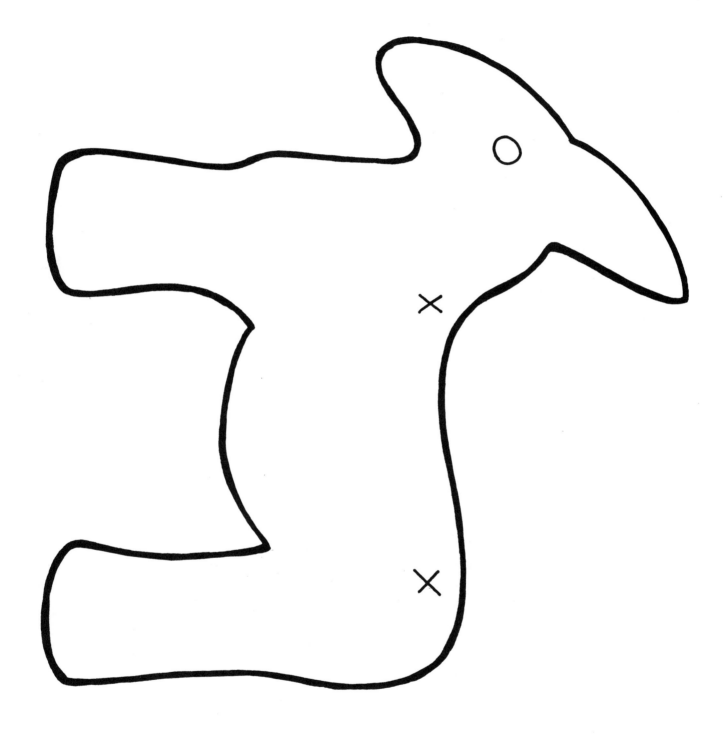

Bark Box

Boxes, baskets, cups, and utensils were crafted from birch bark because it is waterproof and resists decay. Some of the items were decorated with flowers or animals. The ancestors of the Chippewa and Cree Indian tribes made many birch bark containers for daily use.

Materials Needed

- ☐ pattern on page 99
- ☐ newspaper
- ☐ tan (light brown) tagboard
- ☐ glue
- ☐ markers or crayons
- ☐ pencil
- ☐ scissors

Directions

1. Cut a complete pattern for the bark box from newspaper.
2. Use the pattern to cut the box from tagboard.
3. Add pencil lines to the right side of the tagboard to represent the bark. Add marker lines around the edge to represent stitching. If you wish, draw an animal in dark brown on the front of the box.
4. Fold and glue the sides together as shown.

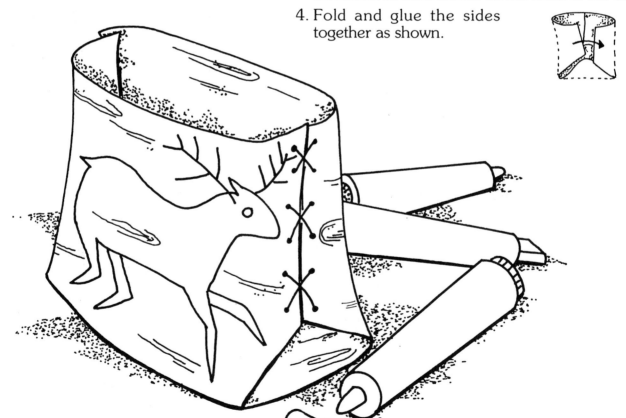

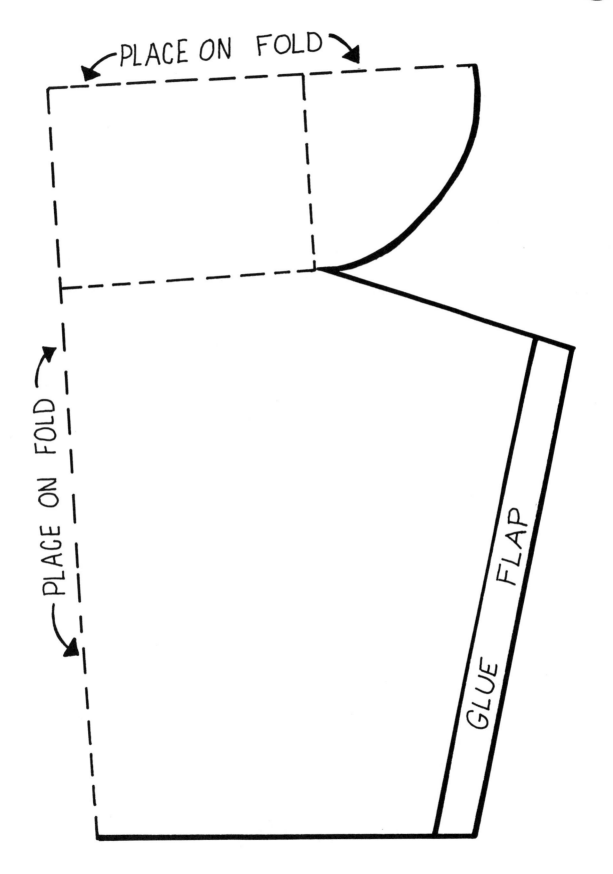

Bark Cloth

Bark cloth is made and used in several parts of the world. Mexican bark cloth is painted with pictures of brightly-colored flowers and birds. To make the cloth, the bark is peeled off the tree, soaked, and pounded until smooth. Bark cloth is light brown in color.

Materials Needed

- ❐ large, brown paper bag
- ❐ colored chalk, markers, or crayons
- ❐ pencil
- ❐ scissors
- ❐ paper towels
- ❐ large bowl of water

Directions

1. Crumple the paper bag and soak it in water for about ten minutes. Squeeze out the water, flatten the bag, and allow it to dry on paper towels.

2. Measure and cut a piece about 12" x 18" (305 x 457 cm) from the paper bag.

3. With your pencil, draw a picture of a flower or animal. Outline the shapes with a black marker.

4. Color the picture with colored chalk that is slightly damp, markers, or crayons. Note: To use chalk, soak the end of the chalk piece in water until it is soft, and then color the picture. Continue wetting the chalk until the picture is finished.

Bird Molas

Molas is a style of appliqué done by the women of Panama. The designs are created by cutting through layers of colored fabric, exposing the colors underneath the top layer. Molas are usually made into wall hangings.

Materials Needed

- ❏ felt scraps in three bright colors
- ❏ 8" x 10" (203 x 254 mm) piece of white fabric
- ❏ a black felt square
- ❏ sharp scissors
- ❏ craft glue
- ❏ straight pins
- ❏ pattern on page 102
- ❏ heavy cardboard (for a frame)
- ❏ stapler
- ❏ hole punch and string (optional)

Directions

1. Choose one of the bird patterns and pin it to the black felt square. (You may wish to enlarge the pattern before positioning it on the felt.)
2. Cut out the bird and glue it to the center of the white fabric. Allow it to dry.
3. Add strips and spots cut from the colored felt to make designs as shown in the illustrations. Glue several different colors on top of each other. (Be sure each piece is smaller than the one underneath it.) Allow the glue to dry.
4. Staple the finished molas to a cardboard frame. *Optional:* Punch holes in the frame and hang it by string.

Butterfly

In early autumn, huge swarms of monarch butterflies migrate south from the United States to Mexico.

Materials Needed

- ☐ waxed paper
- ☐ iron
- ☐ ends of old crayons
- ☐ scissors
- ☐ yarn
- ☐ newspaper

Directions

1. Grate the crayons into fine pieces. Keep each color separate if you wish.
2. Arrange the crayon shavings into the shape of a butterfly on the waxed paper.
3. Cover the crayons with another piece of waxed paper.
4. Place the waxed paper between the pages of newspaper. Carefully press the paper with a medium hot iron until the crayons have melted and the colors are mixed.
5. Cut around the shape, attach the yarn, and hang the butterfly in your window.

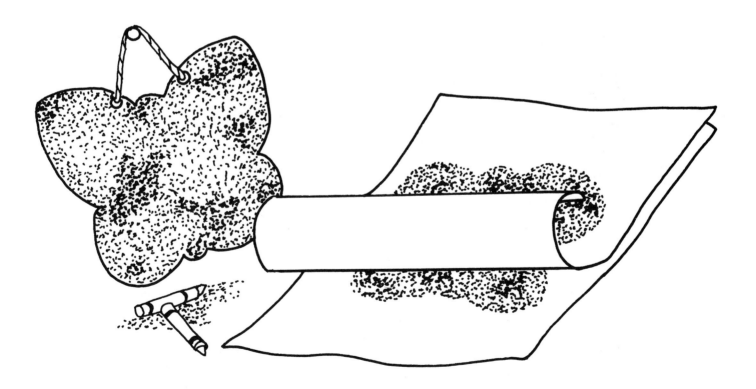

Clan Totem

The Indians of the Northwest (Tlinget, Salish, Haida, Tsimshian, Kwakiutl, Bella Coola, and Nootka) used very tall red cedar trees to carve beautiful totem poles that showed something of the history of their families. Having a totem in front of your house was a sign of family wealth and status. Specific emblems were carved and painted usually in red, blue, black, and green on the totem to tell a story. The following symbols were common: bear, thunderbird, eagle, raven, beaver, killer whale, seal, wolf, and halibut.

Materials Needed

- ❏ cardboard tube (paper towel)
- ❏ cardboard pieces cut from boxes, other cardboard scraps
- ❏ sharp scissors
- ❏ glue, pencil, tape
- ❏ tempera paints, paintbrush, newspaper
- ❏ reference books

Directions

1. Cut four slots in the bottom of the cardboard tube. Cut four "feet" from cardboard and insert them to allow the tube to stand alone.

2. Research your design and then draw it in pencil on the tube. To add dimension, cut 2–4 shapes from the scrap cardboard.

3. Insert the pieces in the slots you have cut in the sides of the tube. Tape them firmly in place inside the tube.

4. Paint your totem pole.

Dream Catcher

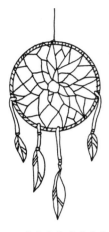

The Ojibwa Indian ancestors believed that good dreams are the source of all wisdom. Children going to sleep were encouraged to dream and remember their dreams. The Ojibwa weaved dream catchers to protect their children from bad dreams. They believed that the good dreams float through the hole in the center of the web and down onto the sleeping child.

Materials Needed

- ☐ plastic lid (at least 6" or 152 mm in diameter)
- ☐ sharp scissors
- ☐ hole punch
- ☐ yarn
- ☐ feathers and beads

Directions

1. Cut the center out of the plastic lid leaving about an inch (25 mm) circular border.

2. Punch holes around the edge of the hoop.

3. Weave the yarn in and out of the holes to make an irregular web in the center of the hoop.

4. Add beads and feathers to make an interesting design. *Note:* Be sure the center feather is hanging the furthest from the bottom of the frame.

5. Attach a yarn hanger, and hang the dream catcher above your bed. Sweet dreams!

Feather Toss

Before North America was settled by Europeans, Native Americans enjoyed playing games. They were fierce competitors and disgraced by injury. Many of the games were designed to develop skills necessary for battle.

Materials Needed

- ❏ a long feather (10" or 254 mm in length)
- ❏ modeling clay
- ❏ markers
- ❏ chalk

Directions

1. Place a small ball of clay (as a weight) on the end of the feather. If several children are playing, mark each feather with a different color for easy identification.

2. Draw a chalk circle on the playground or scratch one in the dirt with a stick.

How to Play

1. Decide on a location from which to throw.

2. Throw the feather, trying to get the weighted end into the circle.

3. The winner is the player whose feather comes closest to the circle.

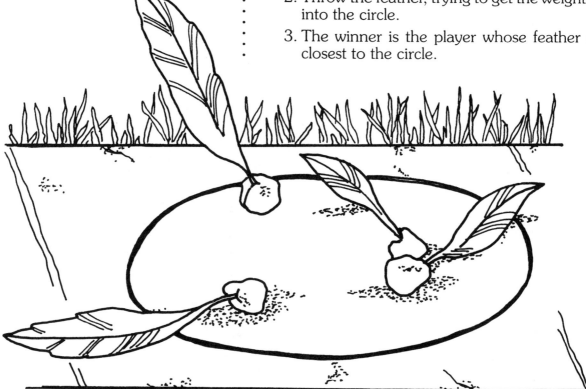

Finger Masks

Inuit women dancers wear these little finger masks. They wave their hands and move their fingers as they dance to rhythmic music. Masks are used in traditional ceremonies and festivals.

Materials Needed

- ☐ scraps of light colored construction paper
- ☐ glue
- ☐ scissors
- ☐ craft materials (yarn scraps, sequins, glitter), seeds
- ☐ crayons or markers

Directions

1. Copy the mask pattern onto construction paper.
2. Design a funny face in the center.
3. Decorate the mask with yarn, sequins, glitter, and/or seeds.
4. Cut out the shape. If desired, fringe and curl the hair.
5. Glue a finger loop onto the back.
6. Design your own finger masks.

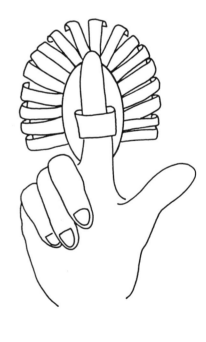

God's Eye

Children in South America might receive god's eyes on their birthdays. The "eye" is begun at birth and a new color is added for each year of life until the child is five.

Materials Needed

☐ two 6–8" (152 x 203 mm) sticks
☐ thin wire
☐ several colors of yarn scraps
☐ scissors
☐ colored beads, glue (optional)

Directions

1. Cross the two sticks at their centers and then bind them together with the wire. Be sure they are held securely.

2. Knot the end of one color of yarn at the center point of the sticks. Wrap the yarn around each arm as shown. Build up the yarn in the center until there is a rounded hump (this is the "eye").

3. Knot a new color onto the end and continue wrapping.

4. Start each new color with another knot.

Optional: Glue beads to the ends of the sticks.

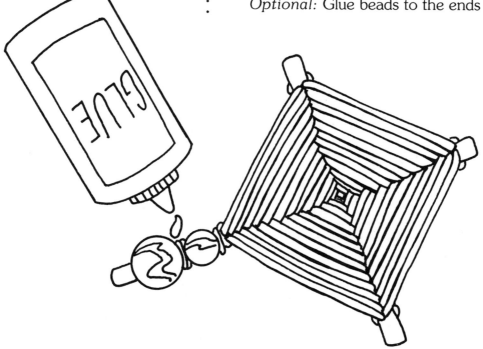

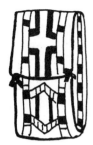

Indian Pouch

During daily life of Native American ancestors, members of every Indian tribe carried bags or pouches. They were made of skins and decorated with traditional motifs. The Plains Indians used belt pouches decorated with geometric designs. The Woodland Indians decorated their pouches with flower designs. The pouches were used to carry necessary items for daily life.

Materials Needed

- ☐ 8" x 10" (203 x 254 mm) light colored felt
- ☐ darning needle, thread
- ☐ sharp scissors
- ☐ markers or fabric paint
- ☐ pattern on page 111

Directions

1. Cut the felt according to the pattern. Cut slits in the back panel of the pouch.
2. Fold in half through the center.
3. Stitch around three sides as shown, leaving the top open.
4. Fringe the top flap.
5. Use markers to decorate the finished pouch with traditional designs.
6. Slip the pouch on your belt.

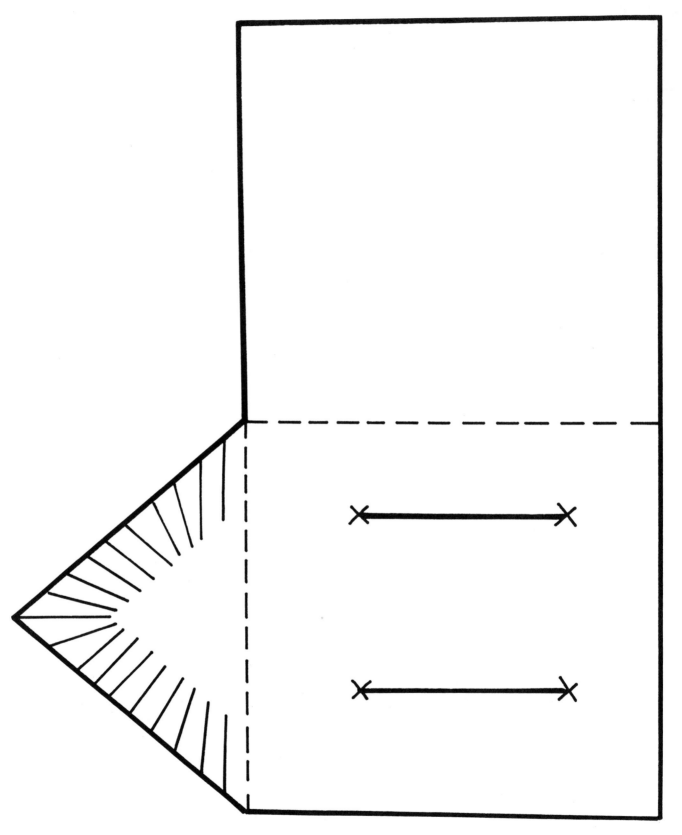

Kachina Doll

The Pueblo Indians believe that kachinas are the living spirits of much loved ancestors. Each spring kachinas come down from the sacred mountain and enter the bodies of men. These men parade as masked figures through the village. They may be dressed as animals, birds, or clowns. The people believe the kachinas will bring spring rains to make the crops grow. Dolls are made to help teach the children about the kachinas.

Materials Needed

- ☐ cardboard tube, 6" (152 mm) in length
- ☐ red, yellow, blue, green, and black paper scraps
- ☐ scissors
- ☐ glue
- ☐ crayons, colored pencils
- ☐ pattern on page 112

Directions

1. Cut a 2" (51 mm) square from red paper. Draw eyes, nose, mouth, and hair.
2. Round the corners of the square and glue in place on the front of the tube near the top.
3. Cut a 4" x 5" (102 x 127 mm) piece of yellow paper to cover the rest of the doll. Glue it in place on the tube.
4. Add decorations of brightly colored paper scraps.
5. Design a headdress (or feathers) for your doll from the colored paper. Use several colors and glue them in layers.
6. Cut a slit in each side of your tube at the top and insert the finished headdress.

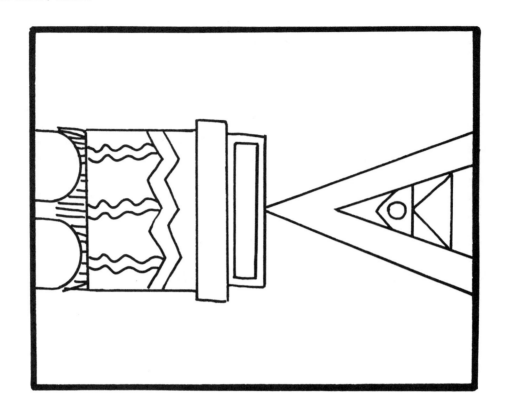

Kinara

The *kinara* holds seven candles, one for each day of Kwanzaa. The black candle in the center stands for the color of the African skin. Three red candles on the left are reminders of past and present struggles, and three green candles on the right represent hope for a prosperous future. On the first night of Kwanzaa, the black candle is lit. After that, one candle is lit each night, alternating red and green.

*M*aterials *N*eeded

- ☐ cardboard egg carton
- ☐ scissors
- ☐ craft glue
- ☐ project clay (p. 4)
- ☐ red, green, and black paint
- ☐ paintbrush
- ☐ three red, one black, and three green candles

*D*irections

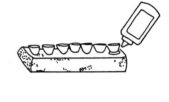

1. Cut the lid off the egg carton. Cut seven egg cups from the inside.
2. Space the egg cups evenly and glue them to the top of the lid.
3. Cover the entire prepared lid with project clay. Allow the clay to dry for several days.
4. Paint the kinara with green, red, and black designs.
5. Insert the candles when the project is completely dry. Place the kinara on the mkeka. (See page 117).

Luminarias

These traditional festival lights began as small bonfires lighting the way to Midnight Mass on Christmas Eve. Some people believed that the Christ Child wandered about during the night blessing the homes of those who set out a guiding light.

Materials Needed

- ❏ several small white paper bags
- ❏ watercolor paints or markers (optional)
- ❏ one cup of sand per bag
- ❏ one votive candle per bag
- ❏ hole punch

Directions

1. Fold down the top of the bag so that it is 4"–5" (102 x 127 mm) high.
2. Paint or draw a design on the front of each bag if desired.
3. Punch small holes with the hole punch to allow light to shine through the bag.
4. Put a cup of sand in each bag.
5. Push the candle into the sand so that it is anchored.

Things to Remember

✔ Keep small children away from the lit candles.
✔ Set the luminarias far enough apart to prevent them from touching.
✔ Allow the candles to burn themselves out.
✔ Do not try to set out luminarias in rain or snow.

Maize

For many Native American ancestors, corn was a primary part of their diet, along with fish and game. It was usually planted in hills with beans so that the vines could be supported by the corn stalks.

Materials Needed

- ❑ project clay (p. 4)
- ❑ yellow, orange, red, and brown paint
- ❑ craft stick
- ❑ green crepe paper
- ❑ scissors
- ❑ paintbrush
- ❑ clear adhesive tape

Directions

1. Shape the clay into a small ear of corn.
2. Use the craft stick to mark kernels in the clay.
3. Alow the ear to dry for several days.
4. Paint the corn yellow or show multicolored kernels.
5. Allow the paint to dry.
6. Cut the crepe paper into husks. Tape the husks at the bottom of the ear of corn.

Mkeka

The mkeka is the place mat upon which the symbols of Kwanzaa are placed. It symbolizes the African tradition. Kwanzaa is a celebration of African cultural heritage.

Materials **N**eeded

- ☐ 12" x 18" (305 x 457 mm) white construction paper
- ☐ red, green, and black paint
- ☐ paintbrushes
- ☐ several vegetables (potato, carrot, pepper)
- ☐ table knife
- ☐ 4" (102 mm) square heavy cardboard
- ☐ sharp scissors

Directions

1. Cut the vegetables to use as stamps. If you wish to include comb painting, cut several notches in one end of the cardboard.
2. Choose one color and paint a border around the paper.
3. Use the paints and stamps to print a pattern on the placemat or use the cardboard "comb" to paint a design.
4. Choose a different color and repeat the procedure.
5. Continue until the place mat is covered. Allow it to dry flat.

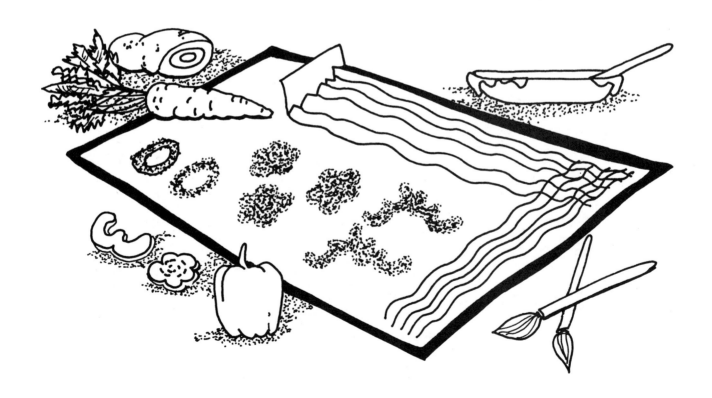

Piñata

These popular decorations may be made in a variety of shapes and are displayed during Christmas and birthday parties. During the celebration, blindfolded children try to hit the piñata and break it open so that the treats can be shared by all.

Materials Needed

- ❏ two brown paper grocery bags
- ❏ scissors
- ❏ glue, masking tape
- ❏ stapler
- ❏ yellow tissue paper
- ❏ black marker
- ❏ wrapped hard candy
- ❏ 15" (381 mm) length of strong cord (for hanging)

Directions

1. Cut two identical circles from the paper grocery bags.
2. Cut the tissue paper into flower petals (see diagram).
3. Glue the petals around the edge of one paper circle, overlapping them if necessary.
4. Use a marker to draw seeds on the other paper circle.
5. Glue and staple the edge of the seed circle onto the circle with petals, leaving an opening at the top.
6. Fill the piñata with hard candy. Tape the hanging cord firmly in place at the top. Glue and staple the piñata closed.

Rainstick

The rainstick is used to imitate the sound of falling rain. A Chilean will work with a hollowed-out cactus and pound cactus thorns into the shaft. Then small pebbles are dropped into the shaft before it is sealed. To hear the sound of falling rain, just shake the stick.

Materials Needed

- ☐ large cardboard tube for gift wrap
- ☐ thumb tacks
- ☐ dry beans or rice
- ☐ recycled aluminum pie tin
- ☐ scissors
- ☐ masking tape
- ☐ paint

Directions

1. Stick the thumb tacks into the tube.

2. To cover the ends of the tube, cut two circles from the aluminum pie tins. Each circle should have a diameter 2" (51 mm) larger than the end of the tube.

3. Cut slits in the circle as shown, fold, and tape it securely to close **one** end of the tube.

4. Pour a small amount of rice or beans inside the tube.

5. Follow step 3 to seal the open end with the remaining aluminum circle. *Note:* Shake or flip the rainstick to make sounds. If needed, add more beans or rice to make the sound louder or longer in duration.

6. Decorate your rainstick by painting interesting designs on it. Allow the paint to dry.

7. Have fun experimenting with several ways to make sounds.

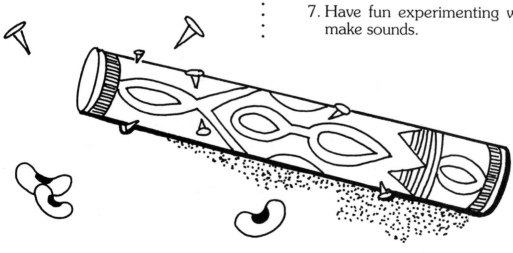

Native American

Sandpainting

Navajo ancestors created their sandpaintings as part of a healing ceremony. The paintings were made directly on the floor of their homes and were destroyed at the end of the ceremony. Different designs were used during the ceremony for bringing rain. Today, the sun is still used in traditional artwork of many Native American and South American cultures.

Materials Needed

- ☐ natural sand
- ☐ cardboard
- ☐ scissors
- ☐ ruler, protractor
- ☐ powdered tempera paint
- ☐ paper cups
- ☐ plastic spoons
- ☐ small paintbrushes
- ☐ glue

Directions

1. Cut the cardboard into a circle.
2. Draw a sun or another appropriate design on the circle.
3. Mix a bit of sand with powdered paint in a paper cup until you reach the desired color. Prepare several colors of sand.
4. Look at your picture and plan where to place each of the colors.
5. Paint a light coating of glue on one section of the sun. Cover the wet glue with one color of sand. Allow to dry.
6. Shake off any excess sand.
7. Continue the process until you have completed all sections.

*P*ictograph *S*croll

Early Native Americans developed ways to record facts and ideas with symbols. The signs were understood by members of the same tribe. Picture writing was done by artists to indicate what they had seen or heard. Some were used only as decorations.

*M*aterials *N*eeded

- ❏ a large brown paper bag or butcher paper
- ❏ two 12" (305 mm), straight, heavy sticks
- ❏ glue or yarn and hole punch
- ❏ markers or colored chalk
- ❏ water in small bowl
- ❏ chart on page 121
- ❏ paper towels

*D*irections

1. Crumple the paper and soak it in water for about ten minutes.

2. Squeeze out the water and flatten the paper. Allow it to dry overnight on paper towels.

3. Plan a story using picture writing symbols. You may need to invent some symbols of your own. Draw the story with markers on your prepared paper.

4. Tear the edges of the paper around the finished story.

5. Glue the left and right edges of the paper securely around the sticks or punch holes in the top and bottom and attach to the sticks with yarn.

6. Hang the finished scroll or roll the sticks inward toward the center.

Stick Slide Game

This game was played by Native American women for recreation. The playing pieces were carved from sticks or straight bones. Lines that represented lightning and dots for rain were etched on the sticks. One stick was known as Four Directions.

Materials Needed

- ❏ four craft sticks
- ❏ red, blue, and black markers
- ❏ 12 toothpicks

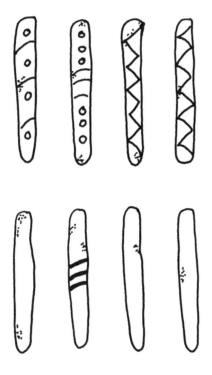

Directions

1. Use the markers to decorate the sticks (see diagram).

How to Play

1. The two players sit facing each other.
2. The first player holds the sticks vertically with the ends touching the ground. She slides her hand out and drops the sticks in front of her.
3. The score is determined by how the sticks fall (see diagram). The player takes one counting stick (toothpick) for each point of her throw.
4. She continues play until she has a throw with no points.
5. Then the play goes to her opponent.
6. The game may end in an agreed number of rounds, or continue with players taking each other's counting sticks when the pile has been exhausted.
7. The player with the most counting sticks at the end of the game is the winner.

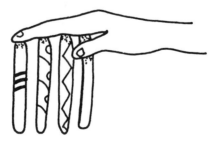

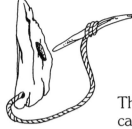

Toss and Catch Game

The Indians of North America used a thin bone awl on which they caught hollow bones to play this game. The Inuit called the game *ajagag*.

Materials Needed

- ☐ a new, sharpened pencil
- ☐ 15" (381 mm) length of string or yarn
- ☐ crayons
- ☐ hole punch
- ☐ 3" x 5" (76 x 127 mm) index card
- ☐ scissors

Directions

1. Draw an eagle (or another traditional symbol) on the index card. Color it and cut out the shape.
2. Make a large hole in the center of the shape.
3. Punch a small hole near an edge of the shape, and tie one end of the yarn securely to the figure. Tie the other end of the yarn to the eraser end of the pencil.

How to Play

The object of the game is to toss and catch the figure on the sharpened end of the pencil. Each player should have five tosses per turn.

Wampum

Before there was money as we know it, the ancestors of the Algonquin and Iroquois tribes used belts and necklaces made of shells for trading. Wampum was used as gifts to seal peace treaties and trade agreements.

Materials **N**eeded

- ❒ white and purple tagboard
- ❒ aluminum foil and silver glitter
- ❒ project clay (p. 4)
- ❒ toothpicks
- ❒ yarn
- ❒ hole punch
- ❒ glue
- ❒ scissors
- ❒ stapler

Directions

Belt:

1. Cut seven to ten circles (3" or 76 mm in diameter) from the white and purple tagboard.
2. You may decorate the circles with foil or glitter.
3. Cut each circle through to the center, form a slight cone and staple in place.
4. Use a hole punch to make two holes in each side of the cones.
5. Thread the cones, alternating purple and white, onto a double length of yarn, leaving about 12" (305 mm) of yarn on the ends for tying.

Necklace:

1. Shape six beads about 1" (25 mm) in diameter from the clay.
2. Insert a toothpick through the center and twist it to enlarge the hole.
3. Allow the beads to dry overnight.
4. You may wish to wrap the dry beads in aluminum foil ("silver").
5. Cut five shell shapes from the white and purple tagboard. Decorate them with silver glitter.

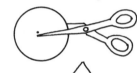

6. Use the hole punch to make two holes at the top of each shell.
7. String your finished pieces, alternating beads and shells, onto a length of yarn.

Weaving

Around the world crafts people weave baskets, clothing, and rugs from a variety of materials. The Navajo people are known for weaving beautiful, bold geometric designs.

Materials Needed

- ☐ 12" x 18" (305 x 457 mm) black construction paper (laminated if possible)
- ☐ scissors
- ☐ tape or glue
- ☐ materials for weaving (raffia, yarn, string, strips of colored paper, and fabric in bright reds, yellows, greens)
- ☐ reference books on weavings

Directions

1. Refer to pictures to examine the interesting designs used in traditional weavings.
2. Fold the black paper in half.
3. Make parallel cuts about 1" (25 mm) apart down the length of the paper from the fold, stopping about 2" (51 mm) from the edge. *Note:* These cuts need not be even or straight. The weave will be more interesting if they are not.
4. Open the black paper.
5. Begin weaving (over and under) to create a design. Remember to alternate each line (under and over). Push the woven pieces down so that the entire cut section is filled.
6. When the weaving is completed, turn over the black paper and glue or tape the loose ends in place.

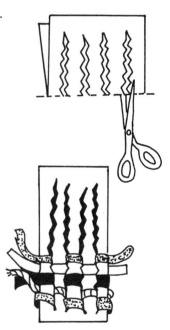

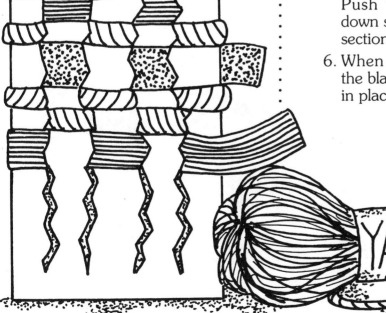

Worry Dolls

The children of Central America tell their worries to these dolls before going to bed each night. The dolls are then placed under their pillows, and by morning the children believe all their problems will be solved!

Materials Needed

- ☐ large wooden bead
- ☐ one 9" (229 mm) chenille stem
- ☐ one 4" (102 mm) chenille stem
- ☐ masking tape
- ☐ yarn in several bright colors
- ☐ scissors
- ☐ fineline permanent black marker

Directions

1. Insert the long chenille stem through the bead. Fold it in half and twist to make the neck of the doll.

2. Fold the short chenille stem in half and attach just below the neck. This will become the doll's arms.

3. Use the marker to draw hair and a face on the bead.

4. Starting at the neck, add masking tape to form the shoulders and torso of the body.

5. Wrap yarn carefully around the entire doll, turning up the ends of the chenille stems to form hands and feet.

Woven Basket

Basketry has been a popular craft around the world for many years. The baskets of some early Native American tribes were made from natural material, like twigs, bark, leaves, or grass. The basket maker either coiled or twined the materials to make the baskets. The coiled baskets were woven so tightly that they were used for carrying water.

Materials Needed

- ☐ clean cardboard container having a 5" (127 mm) base and sides
- ☐ scissors
- ☐ heavy string or yarn

Directions

1. Cut the sides of your cardboard container into 1" (25 mm) strips, leaving the bottom intact.

2. Begin at the bottom of the container, weaving the yarn or string over and under the side strips until you are within an inch of the top. *Note:* This is somewhat like the twining method.

3. Fold the top of the cardboard strips into the basket and tuck them into the weaving. Tie a knot and cut the string.

Zuni Basket Game

Native American ancestors played several games using bowls or baskets and painted pebbles or peach stones. They often gambled personal items on the outcome of the games.

Materials Needed

- ☐ basket or flat bowl (about 10" or 254 mm in diameter)
- ☐ heavy white cardboard
- ☐ scissors
- ☐ colored marker

Directions

1. Cut the cardboard into five 1½" (38 mm) squares.
2. Color a design on **one side** of each square.

How to Play

1. Any number of players sit facing each other in a circle.
2. Each player in turn throws the squares up from the basket and catches them.
3. Points are tallied by counting how the squares land (see scoring below).
4. The winner is the first player to have ten points.

Scoring:

Five painted sides = 10 points
Five plain sides = 5 points
Four plain sides = 4 points
Three plain sides = 3 points
Two plain sides = 2 points
One plain side = 1 point